NORTH
SEA

Groningen .

Egmond
aan Zee

. Alkmaar

.Zwolle

.Amsterdam

THE NETHERLANDS

Schenveningen

Amersfoort .

.The Hague

.Arnham

.Rotterdam

GERMANY

BELGIUM

. BRUSSELS

.Valkenburg

NIGHT ISLAND

BY

JOHANNA VAN LEEUWEN SEPE

WingSpan Press

Published in the United States and the United Kingdom
by WingSpan Press, Livermore, CA

The WingSpan name, logo and colophon are the trademarks of
WingSpan Publishing.

ISBN 978-1-59594-613-3 (pbk.)
ISBN 978-1-59594-930-1 (ebk.)

First edition 2017

Printed in the United States of America

www.wingspanpress.com

Library of Congress Control Number: 2017954410

1 2 3 4 5 6 7 8 9 10

I dedicate this book to my editor Beth De Feo. Without her expertise I don't think I could have done this.

I also want to thank my family, who gave me the courage to write my story.

I am grateful to all my former colleagues who without knowing, helped me cope with my past and who made me who I am today. Most of all I am thankful to have discovered dance. Without it, I don't know what would have happened to me.

"You wanted to belong. The problem was, no matter how well you kept your secret, the very fact of having one was enough to separate you from everyone else."

— Lisa Kleypas, *Rain Shadow Road*

"Secrets affect you more than you'd think. You lie to keep them hidden. You steer talk away from them. You worry someone'll discover yours and tell the world. You think you are in charge of the secret, but isn't it the secret who's actually using you"?

— David Mitchell, *Black Swan Green*

"Nothing weights on us so heavily as a secret."

— Jean de la Fontaine

CONTENTS

NIGHT ISLAND

ONE

Looking Back

Motionless on a street in The Hague, I stand staring at a building I haven't seen in a long time. It looks different, yet the same. A sign informs me that this place currently houses an insurance agency. I wonder how many businesses this building has seen come and go over the years. I'm sure they all have a story to tell, good or bad. Now the large street level windows have blinds which are lowered. It doesn't matter though, I know exactly what it looks like.

When I close my eyes, I see my parents rushing around serving their customers. I see myself, a small child, playing with my dolls under a billiard table. I hear the patrons chatting about their day, laughing and enjoying each other's company.

I know I will never return to this place that houses my childhood memories like a photo album housing its photos. I'm having a difficult time removing myself. I just want to stand here a little longer and reminisce for a while.

This is my homeland, where the happiest, saddest, and most terrifying moments of my life took place. It is where I discovered the pleasure of dance. These memories are clouded over when I recall Papa and Mom speaking in hushed tones. Soon I hear other voices belonging to our neighbors and friends. I witness them taking our belongings, the billiard tables, the bar, and various pieces of furniture. I feel the pulse of adrenaline as Mom and I, race to seek shelter as fighter planes soar overhead.

I shake myself from that scene, but soon enough, my thoughts turn to the one thing that guided most of my decisions: to talk to someone new, to approach a young man whom I was interested in, but most of all the fear of someone finding out the truth about me. I try to erase it from my mind as I did so many times before, but the burden I've carried for so long is too dark and heavy. My secret has prevented me from feeling worthy of respect and love. I emerge from my memories like a swimmer coming up for air.

After all these years, I know it's time to be free of my secret. I believe now that it was never my sin to bear. However the guilt of being closely related to one of the darkest and most shameful periods in history made me feel I had to pay for it.

❦

In 1939, Germany invaded Poland for the start of the greatest war the world had ever known. It was also the year I was born.

My parents owned a café in The Hague, the city where the seat of the Dutch government is located. Our home was an apartment above the café. There was also a large room upstairs for special occasions, such as various clubs meetings and wedding receptions. Downstairs was spacious and full of light. Tables lined the front windows where people routinely savored their morning coffee and enjoyed something to eat. On the right side of the entrance was a dark looking wood bar with some bar stools that I loved to turn on as fast as I could. It was also the spot where I remember seeing my busy mom the most. In the back, there were two billiard tables with large lights hanging over top.

I spent most of the time in the café, playing with my dolls under the billiard tables and running around the place. Mom put food in my mouth on the run. She was concerned about me not eating enough, so she would check on me between customers to see if I'd eaten the last thing she'd popped into my mouth.

On busy days, they didn't have enough eyes to keep track of me. On a very hot summer day, no one noticed me running out the front door in bare feet. I ran onto the metal basement beer and soda delivery doors, and I stood there yelling at the top of my lungs because my feet were burning. I did not do much running for a while after that.

Papa was tall, but not too skinny, with a strong face and brown hair. His name was not too skinny either, Johannes Antonius Augustines van Leeuwen, but everyone called him Jan. He was married before and already had two teenage daughters by the time I came around. He was playful and more happy-go-lucky than my mother was.

Mom and I

Mom was also tall and not too thin, but her name was much shorter, Anna Catharina, Ans for short. I never thought of her as young or beautiful, perhaps because of her strong personality or the fact that she had gray hair. However, when I saw a picture from when she was very young, I finally noticed she had a beautiful face. Mom was thirty-nine when she gave birth to me. At the time, that was considered old to have babies. I do not remember doing much with her when I was very little, perhaps because she was just too busy with the café to spend quality time with me. I had much more interaction with Papa. If Mom could read this right now, she probably would say, "Yes, while I was working like a slave trying to catch up on things, your father would go have fun."

It is more likely that she told Papa to take me with him on his leisure activities so she could get her work done. I remember distinctly a trip to the beach in Scheveningen, were he let me ride on a pony and were I splashed to my heart delight in the North Sea. Those outings were not often, I mostly remember attending boring soccer games or going fishing with him.

Me on a donkey in Scheveningen.

Wherever Papa and I went, it was always on the bike. I would sit in a little seat connected to the handlebars in front, and my Papa would sing to the rhythm of his pedaling. If it started to rain, a frequent occurrence in Holland, we would both sing, "With your nose in the rain, with your nose in the wind." We got soaked to the bone and loved it, until my mother saw us and scolded my father. We went on the bike looking for good fishing spots, sometimes even outside The Hague. When it was time for morning coffee, usually around ten in the morning, no matter where we were in our travels we would go to the nearest farm we could find. Papa would ring the doorbell and ask if he could "buy" a cup of coffee. It always worked! I don't know if they ever made him pay for it, but I do know he loved chatting with the farmers. After coffee and a cookie, it was back on the bike and time to pedal to our fishing spot for the day. Papa did not have fancy fishing gear, just a little red and white float he'd set on the water. The little float going up and down when a fish nibbled on his bait was kind of fun to watch. When nothing happened for longer than five minutes, I lost all interest. On the other hand, papa could stare at it for hours.

On one of our fishing trips, I was picking little buttercups while Papa was talking to a farmer we had met on one of our coffee breaks. I must have drifted farther and farther away, until I realized Papa was nowhere in sight. I asked two older boys who approached me on their bicycles if they knew where my father was. They realized that I was lost and asked me where I lived. I told them in a big house on the Apeldoornselaan. Mom was surprised when I arrived at our house with the two older boys as my escorts. When Papa arrived home his face was as white as a sheet. He asked, "Is Pucky home?" Mom replied that I was not to make him feel guiltier and more upset than he already was. There were not many more fishing trips with Papa after that, which was fine with me and probably fine with him.

Around the time I was four, I got sick with diphtheria. I had a high fever that affected my throat and eyes. Wherever I looked, I saw double. I thought it was quite amusing, as if my eyes had magical powers. The paintings on the walls suddenly had two boats, two houses and two trees. What bothered me very much was when I swallowed food it would not go down. Instead, it just came up through my nose! Naturally, my reaction became fear of putting anything in my mouth. I was a poor eater to begin with, so during this time I went from skinny to just skin and bones.

Mom had no time to nurse me back to health. Thus, she arranged for me to go to a children's rehab home in the country for six weeks. Mom brought me to the railroad station where a stranger put a nametag around my neck. I sat in the train and played with the other children. It was exciting; I did not remember ever being on a train before. The train left and I happily looked out of the windows. There was so much to see! Reality set in quickly once we got off the train and I realized Mom was not there.

In attempt to assuage my anxiety, I quickly asked the nearest adult where my Mother was and when I would be seeing her again. I was comforted with the reply that she would be coming for me soon and that I was not to worry. This same adult drove me and some other children to the rehab home. Again no sight of Mom. I questioned her again but was told the same response. Homesickness overcame me and I was concerned I would never see my parents again. I was devastated that Mom left me there with those strangers. It was a different time and, I suppose, that was the way things were done.

I desperately clung to Antje, the little doll Mom had given me at the beginning of the trip. I would talk to her all the time and felt we were in this together. Antje was the biggest comfort to me, my link to home, a patient listener and something to cuddle with at night when I felt most homesick.

The food was a thick, beige colored lumpy concoction. It was probably oatmeal but my childhood recollection was a horrid slop. Because of the illness, I still had problems swallowing and the food, needless to say, made me gag. The nurses thought I did not like it so they made me sit there with the word "eat" thrown at me repeatedly. After a while everyone would be gone except the beige stuff and me. I was punished numerous times and was put in my crib for what seemed like hours. After a while, there was some improvement in my eating since I forced myself to swallow the beige slop. I guess they had taught me a lesson.

I spent hours in that crib since we were required to nap during the day. Out of frustration, I would jump repeatedly until eventually falling asleep from pure exhaustion. Of course, I got in trouble for that too. There were roughly ten cribs in a large, white room. Everything from the nurses, to the walls, floor, cribs, sheets, blankets, and even chamber pots, were as white as freshly fallen snow.

Antje and my thumb were my comforts during this difficult time away from home. Not only was I a thumb-sucker but I would pick wool from my blanket and run it in a circle around my nose while thumbing. This too was not allowed and sadly, they took my fuzz away. I needed that fuzz more than ever so I hid my new fuzz under the mattress. It was good for a while but then I dropped it in the chamber pot with pee and that was the end of it. They punished me once again.

After three weeks, parents were allowed to visit. My Mom took the train to see me, but upon her arrival, she was informed that her visit would not be beneficial to me. I had finally made some progress, so seeing a parent would only upset me and set me back. Mom dutifully listened to those instructions and returned home without seeing me.

Surely, I was not the easiest child there, between my refusals to eat, using the bed like it was a trampoline, and my fuzz making. Many children cried at naptime and at night. I do not think it was a happy place for anybody.

At the end of six weeks, some of the children, including me, were put back on the train with a tag around our neck. This was scary because nobody had told me where I was going now. When I got off the train in The Hague, some children called out "mama" and when I followed them, I saw a small group of women in silhouettes standing on the train station's platform. I had to walk quite far which gave me ample time to figure out if any of those waving silhouettes was my Mom. However, I was too weak to show happiness when I finally spotted her. Although I was lucky to survive diphtheria, Mom could not believe her eyes. I looked worse than when she had put me on that train six weeks prior.

The experience at the rehab center changed me. I distrusted and was overly cautious of all grownups, including my Mom. I feared she would send me away again. It had been done once and I had no guarantee it wouldn't happen again. After all, I never knew why I had to go to that awful place to begin with. Was it because I was a bad girl? Whenever Mom got upset with me, I became terribly worried she would send me back to that "white place."

One morning while I was in the apartment playing with my dolls, I heard music coming from the big room next door. My curiosity got the best of me and was lured to the half-opened doorway. I was pleasantly surprised to see a woman with a group of children moving to beautiful music. This sight intrigued me so much that I found myself kneeling by the door to take it all in. I had never seen anything so lovely before. This woman rented the room to teach rhythmic dancing to a group of little girls a little older than I was. I watched them every time she came, admiring all the things she was teaching the girls. After they left, I tried mimic their dance moves. Naturally, I thought I was really good at it, so when she asked me if I wanted to join them I was thrilled. From that moment on, I was completely hooked on dancing. I didn't just run or walk any longer; instead, I danced all over the café with one of my mother's scarves wrapped around me as a costume, entertaining the café's customers. I hardly knew what a dancer was, but I knew I was one!

Papa and Mom enrolled me in pre-school when I was four. We did the usual things – coloring and drawing – things I was not very good at. At the end of the school year, the class was to perform a fairy dance for the parents. I figured I was going to be much better at that and looked forward to practicing. Unfortunately, I was not chosen to be the lead dancer elf. All the girls had to wear the same costume, made from a white sheet, but the lead girl also wore a pointy hat with a veil to show she was special. At the end of the performance, they took a picture of all of us. The teacher told us to sit on one knee with one hand under the chin. I did not want a picture with the girl who was lead elf. Focused completely on the man with the camera, I glared with disgust as if he was to blame for it all. I put both of my hands balled in tight fists on my knee to look as annoyed by this affair as possible. I was determined to stand out one way or another.

The Elf's Dance. I am sitting on the bottom row, second from left.

Since I was born the year the war started, it did not have an effect on me. After all, this was life as I knew it. There were many people in uniforms around who spoke a different language. They paraded the streets and came into our café. The room upstairs was often full of those uniformed men. They sang and were loud, often keeping me awake until late at night.

However, little by little, things began to change. The woman who gave me rhythmic dance classes did not come anymore, and I missed her. My parents spoke softly to each other with expressions I had not seen before. I saw more of the uniformed people in the café and less of the regular customers. Like our regular customers, things started to disappear as well. The billiard tables were taken away, and the bar was dismantled and dragged out in pieces. Our furniture was soon gone, and in no time only our beds, suitcases, and boxes with our remaining possessions remained. We took these boxes and some suitcases to be stored in different places throughout in the city. I didn't understand what was happening and was very scared.

One of those mornings, I awoke to only Mom. I expected Papa to be back later in the day but he did not come home. Another day passed, and I asked Mom where he was. She said not to worry. This was the first of many vague responses from my mother. The following day, Mom packed individual suitcases for the two of us. Again, I expected my father to come home. I was worried that if we left, he wouldn't know where to find us. My mother again insisted I should not be concerned about Papa's whereabouts. I grabbed my little suitcase where my favorite dolly Antje was tucked securely inside, while Mom slung a backpack onto her shoulders and carried a bigger suitcase. She closed the door and we left. We would never return there. Of course, I didn't know that at the time.

TWO

Mad Tuesday

On Tuesday, September 5, 1944, we walked to the train station. When we arrived, people around us were yelling, spitting, and even throwing stones. It was the strangest thing. My mother and I huddled close to one another and waited for the train. We boarded a train to Valkenburg a town in the south of Holland, along with throngs of people. The hotel we were staying at in Valkenburg was already home to many women and children, some I even recognized from our neighborhood.

Valkenburg. I am sitting on the bottom row, second from left.

When I think of Valkenberg, I recall it as a nice place with children to play with. More specifically, I remember Mom being more attentive to me than ever before. I assume it was because she no longer had the café to manage. I, in turn, relished all the attention. Mom would file and buff my nails until they were shiny and beautiful. What I liked most was our walks up into the mountains. I had never seen mountains before! North Holland, where we were from was as flat as a pancake. Here, the mountains were glorious peaks that poked the fluffy, white clouds and seemed to reached the clouds. Mom got me a walking stick with a Valkenburg emblem on it and I happily zigzagged my way up the mountain with it. I did not know why we were in Valkenberg, to me it was like a vacation. There were new sights, experiences and valued uninterrupted time with Mom. It did not take long for our happy time in Valkenburg to turn into a fearful one. Mom and I were on top of the mountain when suddenly the sky was filled with airplanes. It was a dogfight and we were in the middle of it! I was five and a half years old, and didn't know exactly what was going on, but instinctively knew it was bad. Machine gun fire struck the ground around us as the fighters circled above to get a better angle on each other. Everywhere I turned was either grass, dirt and rocks exploding into the air or the roar and presences of planes. It was total chaos. One plane spiraled down in flames and exploded upon hitting the ground. The impact shook the world around me, the noise was deafening to my small ears in which I quickly clamped my hands over in protection. The smoke was thick and dark, and was choking all my senses.

I never saw Mom so scared. She grabbed my hand and we ran faster than we thought possible. As we descended the mountain we could no longer see the planes because of the trees, but we could still hear them. Unsure of the direction of machine gun or the possibility of another plane crashing we continued running like the wind through the trees and down the steep mountain path. We could see flames through the trees and knew planes had crashed not far from us. Somehow Mom and I survived that tumultuous day on the mountain and walked away unscathed, well at least physically.

Our stay in Valkenburg did not last long. I was fine with leaving this once happy "vacation" spot since there were constant planes overhead and we no longer felt safe. Mom said that we were going to a better place. I wondered if Papa would know where this better place was and questioned my mother. Mom replied, "Don't worry he will see us when he is done. He has to do a lot of work." A few days later, mom and I, as well as a group of women and children from our hotel all boarded a train and arrived in a town called Visselhovede.

From the train station, we ventured to a place that must have been a gym in its better days. A portion of the building had holes in the ceiling; it was messy, dirty and smelled of smoke. In another part of the building which was going to be our home away from home, there was a lot of straw and empty burlap bags. Mom instructed me to help her fill the bags so we had something to sleep on that night. The straw smelled very good, but that evening, much to my surprise, there were many crawling critters ready to attack. I awoke with many bumps and bites, but there was nothing we could do about it. "We just have to deal with it," Mom said.

When it came to food, everyone had to fend for themselves. Mom went to a children's daycare in the little town, where they needed a cook. She secured the job because of her experience running the café. We walked there early in the morning, and while she prepared food, I stayed with the other children but played mostly by myself. The highlight was lunch. There was not much variety in it, but it was heaven for me. Every day I had potatoes with bacon and onions, and that was fine by me, because I loved it. Knowing that there probably would not be much more food the rest of the day, I ate until my stomach hurt. The child who had been such a bad eater was gone forever. The one thing that I detested, but had to do there, was nap with the other children.

Remaining still and quiet for two hours when you are five and a halve years old is not easy, even though the cot was more comfortable than the straw bags we slept on at night.

After some time we packed everything again. Instead of carrying all the clothes in the suitcases, Mom layered my belongings on me, one layer over the next. "It is easier to carry them that way," she said. We traveled in a truck and stayed in a movie theater. This time, the group was smaller. There were about twenty-five of us. The theatre had a narrow stage and was stripped of all its chairs. Vacant in furniture but full of lice. Once it got dark, the tiny mites crawled all over me. I scratched incessantly all night long. When it rained, water ran down some of the walls and made the straw we slept on wet. We tried to find a better spot for our straw bags, but the whole place was smelly, damp and cold. Even the woolen horse blankets that we had were not enough to keep us warm. The old theater was worse than a bad dream, especially since things were just as dreary, dark and disgusting during daytime.

Food became the most important thing in our lives. Mom didn't hold the lunch job for very long. Either the daycare closed or we were now too far away to travel there. Our days became consumed with looking for something to eat. We would walk from farm to farm, propositioning work in exchange for food. Due to the war, men were scarce on the farms, which in turn worked out well for Mom and me. We harvested potatoes, which I found to be fun taking them out of the ground. It was a revelation to unearth them, like opening presents. Sitting on my knees in the dark earth digging next to Mom, was like an unusual game we played together. The potatoes came in all shapes and sizes; I recall proudly showing Mom the biggest ones I found. We dug up potatoes for many days, and in return, the farmers fed us well. The various farm owners gave us potato soup or potatoes with a touch of bacon when we were lucky and some kind of cabbage greens. On our walks, we would also find wild greens that were edible. Mom called it *milde* and *zuring*. The former tasted like spinach and the latter was sour. According to my mother, they were a good source of vitamins and made me stronger. In the evening with our bellies full and day's work behind us, Mom and I lumbered back to our lice-infected quarters only to start all over again come daybreak.

I never understood the reasons why we had to move so often, nor did I question my Mother. This time I was delighted to leave that God-forsaken movie theater. So again all my clothes went on, layer over layer, and we left.

We boarded a truck again and I wondered what our next resting place would be. I didn't have to wonder long because it was not too far from the movie theater. It seemed like it was an abandoned summer camp. Here, more people who, I guess, had been staying at another place before, joined us. Again, we slept on straw bags, but these were on bunk beds. This place was also filthy and damp. It did have a kitchen, so when we were lucky enough to have something to cook we could, and Mom did so many times. I don't know how she got these food items or what she did to get them, but somehow she always managed to have something for me to eat. Although I was miserable, I was never terribly hungry.

The place had biting fleas and rats, and understandably so, I was frightened of them. The fact that we were a little elevated off the floor gave me relief. At least the rats were not walking over me during the darkest hours. When the coughing from my slumbering neighbors would wake me up in the black of night, I would tuck my head under the blanket for protection. I would hear rats scurrying under my bunk bed and wonder how many there were. Thankfully, I didn't see them during the day, but at night the place was theirs. Coping with fleas and lice was enough. I was infested with lice for quite some time, Mom tried to comb the lice out when I complained too much but that did not rid me of the pestering mites. I could feel them crawling all over my head. At night it was especially bad. I often had a hard time falling asleep because those critters would be scampering on my scalp and made me terrible itchy. I scratched so much that it gave me many sores on my scalp.

During this time, death and sickness was all around us. I recall one old lady in our group who had died and I was saddened by it. However, what was most upsetting to me was the illness of a little baby girl. I don't know what illness she had, but her face and body were full of sores. Mom told me that she was very sick and so we'd visit her every day and bring her an egg. The nourishment didn't help. I saw the tiny girl after she died and could not believe my eyes. Like a miracle, all the sores on her face were gone and she looked beautiful. Her mother made a circle of daisies to put on her head and everyone laid daisies all around her little body that was dressed in white. She looked like an angel in her tiny coffin. It was so heart wrenching, I would cry every time I thought of her. I knew death would happen to old people, but it was devastating to realize that it could even happen to a baby, to a Mom, or me.

Mom had heard there was a train stopped in close proximity to where we stayed that contained some kind of grain. When we arrived at the train with some other mothers and children, we heard the thunderous engines of airplanes approaching. Instinctively, we knew it was time to hide and quickly scurried under the train. The planes were directly over us and began bombing the train. We were all terribly frightened in our now unsafe hiding spot. The other children and I yelled as loud as we could to drown out the noise of the planes, but they kept on circling and attacking the train. Seconds seemed like hours to me, but finally this horrific event ended and we were all in one piece and alive.

We quickly realized how lucky we were since many of the other train cars were destroyed. Our silver lining was the large amount of barley we retrieved from the train that day.

On a cold early winter day, Mom and I were walking along a small canal in search of our next meal. I was amusing myself while holding a slender stick in the water pretending to fish like Papa. I remember being fascinated by the little fish swimming in and out of the growth along the water's edge with their little mouths taking quick gulps of air as they surfaced. It reminded me of when Papa and I went fishing, so naturally I inquired again about Papa and whether he was coming to get us and take us home. Of course, Mom replied emphatically that he was fine and I needn't worry.

After our close encounters with enemy planes on the mountain and again the train, I was without a doubt, petrified of airplanes. All day, every day I was constantly listening for the sound of their approach. Mom reassured me not to let fear get the best of me but I could not help myself, it was a part of me.

Our peaceful walk along the water's edge quickly changed when I heard the roar of engines heading our way. Before I could shout, "Let's hide!" Mom had beaten me to it. I guess she had been keeping an ear out, too. She grabbed me by the arm and pulled me into a low bush. The planes were bombing, and I made myself as small as I could with Mom almost on top of me. I held my ears and tried not to hear or think about what was happening. At that moment, I just tried to focus on those tranquil little fish in the water.

I learned to block things out when they were too scary, a kind of self-protection. If I saw something that scared me, I put my hands over my face with my fingers a little bit apart to be able to look through. It made me feel like I was standing behind a fence that would protect me.

We ate whatever we could find, a leftover potato here and a turnip there. Winter was here and nothing was growing anymore. Luckily, there were several farms around us, so we walked and walked searching the fields for some remaining food. It got increasingly difficult to do, as the fields were picked over. On top of that, the ground was frozen and the days and nights were terribly cold.

Mom heard from one of the other women in our group that there was a shoe factory that had been bombed and they thought there might be still some good shoes in the place. Mom emptied her suitcase and backpack and off we went to check it out with a couple of other women. Success! Lucky for us there was an abundance of black patent-leather girl's shoes. Mom packed so many pairs she could hardly move. At one point when we were walking back "home," she fell backwards from the weight, and the other women had to help her back up. They all laughed so long and hard. I could not understand why my mother was so happy.

Our shoe factory finds changed our daily routine in the sense that we would now walk from farm to farm to exchange the shoes for food. Sometimes we would get a little bread and sometimes when we were lucky, a sliver of bacon, but it was mostly eggs. Some cracked as we carried them from one farm to the next. Mom would say, "Here, suck it out of the shell." I ate many raw eggs; they did me more good than harm and got us through that horrible cold winter.

We walked so much every day that I started to get holes in my shoes. The patent-leather shoes were too valuable to put on my feet. It was more important to have a full tummy than dry feet. Mom would put dry newspaper in them in the morning and that had to do.

Many people in our group got sick from cold, hunger and the unsanitary conditions. Mom always gave eggs to sick children or older people that were helpless. Mom dragged me all over the place to keep us from starving, but not everyone was able to do the same or had enough will to do so. I overheard Mom talking with a friend, "They complain we don't share our food, but why don't they take their hands out of their pockets and do something to help themselves." Frustration, hunger, illness and fear were more abundant this winter then I recalled at the beginning of our journey from The Hague.

Tensions were mounting not only amongst the adults but amongst the children as well. There was a lot of bickering going on between us and it was mostly about food. It was Mom's determination to get us food each day that kept us going and for the most part out of trouble.

We were with quite a big group, some women alone and others with children. The children were mostly boys whom I didn't care for. They were very tough and, in my eyes, mean. They would always try to catch me or spit on me, which bothered me a lot. On one of those occasions I was so angry, I picked up stones and threw them at the boys to defend myself. I hit one of them and they went running to their mother to complain. Mom found out and made me apologize to those bullies, and, on top of that, I had to give them two eggs. I was not happy that she made me do this and I walked over to them in anger. After that, they teased me even more, taunting me to throw stones so they could get more eggs.

Some buildings that I would see on our walks in the town had big holes in them without roofs. I could look right through them and see day light. They had been bombed, but to me, they reminded me of my dollhouse back home. Some had no front walls, and you could see all the rooms and there was even some furniture left against a wall on a higher floor. Everything was a mess with rubble all over the place. Mom and I were a mess, too, and I itched all over.

After a few attempts to get an answer from my mom, I no longer questioned where Papa was. He was just not there, and, since what surrounded me was so bizarre, my mind was simply on surviving and not on his whereabouts. I stayed very close to Mom when we were traveling around. My frequent thought was, *if I lose her, what would I do.* She was all I had, and the only one who knew how to get out of here and get us back home. I had no idea where I was. *Would anyone know where the Apeldoornselaan was, where I used to live? How would I get there?*

How long we stayed in each place is hard to recall. Time is meaningless when you are a child. To me, even though I remembered my home and wanted to get back there, it seemed we had been living in this strange manner for a very, very long time. I turned six that January, but there was no celebration.

THREE

Liberation

A carefree life, filled with simple pleasures and dancing felt like a lifetime ago. In actuality, eight months had past, and for a young child birthdays are how we remember those early years. My most recent birthday was full of fear and angst for what the future held. I had matured in a sense that I saw, felt, and comprehended feelings that are more complex; sadness, hunger and pain. This was the life I was accustomed to now, nomadic, wartime traveling with my Mom. Each day was an unknown, and each day I hoped for better.

A sudden excitement arose within our group. Instinctively, I knew it was a happy excitement. Trucks full of soldiers arrived one after another like a parade. Everybody was laughing and hugging. These contrasted the ones I remembered from our café, through uniforms, language and overall demeanor. They set up numerous substantial tents and doled out cots and blankets. Blankets that I can still smell today because they were fresh and clean, something that had become foreign to us in the past year. I remember the soldiers inviting all of us children to come inside one of the bigger tents. Apprehensive at first but excited all the same, we entered the safe haven. We were thrilled to see the long tables covered with cups of milk and large thick slices of white bread smothered with butter and red jam. I looked at what was sitting in front of me and could not remember ever seeing anything so delicious. This bread tasted like heaven- on- earth, and I never tasted that particular combination of flavors before or since.

The soldier's voices were kind, but foreign to my ear. When they spoke with Mom, I realized they were foreign to her as well. It didn't matter. They sounded very friendly and everyone was grinning ear to ear. Mom said the soldiers were from a faraway place called Canada and that they had traveled very far to assist us.

Joy and laughter was returning to our camp and among "our" people. One of Mom's friends liked the soldiers so much she kissed one of them! I loved them, too. They gave us delicious chocolates and crackers, and Mom smoked cigarettes again. Even though it had been raining for days and everything around us, including my feet, was muddy; for me the sun was shining now. There would be no more trouble. We were finally going home. It meant no more roaming around with wet cold feet or being surrounded by mean kids, but most importantly no more anxiety and sheer terror of loud airplanes, bombs, and explosions. Mom and I were given back hope, normalcy and hopefully happiness again. We were going back to the café and I would see all my dollies and toys again. Maybe the woman who gave the dance lessons would be back, too. I looked forward to seeing everything as I remembered, a warm place that smelled good and where nothing bad would happen.

A few days after the soldiers arrived, we piled into trucks and headed back to The Hague. The first thing we did when we got back was go to the people who were holding our clothes and other belongings. We went to three houses, and each time they told Mom they no longer had our things. At one house, we rang the bell but when the door opened, the woman yelled at Mom from the top of the stairs to close the door and go away. I thought this was somewhat rude. Mom said that the reason why we didn't get our things back was that they didn't like us. She didn't explain what we had done to make them dislike us. That was something I didn't understand. I had not been that naughty; I just threw a couple of stones when I was angry.

Of course, now I can make sense of it all. Our possessions were things they could barter for food. The winter of 1944 – 45 was the last winter of the war, and they refer to it as the "hunger winter" in the Netherlands. Many people died from cold and starvation.

After those former friends rejected us, we had to register ourselves with the Dutch government. We went to fill out papers. I was bored stiff because everything took hours. When we were finally done, we walked to a bathhouse. We undressed and stood naked in the back of a long line of barren people. To see all those women and children totally exposed was strange to me. I had never even seen Mom naked before, and here were people of all shapes and sizes, even a woman with a big belly. I think she was pregnant and I couldn't keep my eyes off her, she looked so bizarre to me. The children gawked at each other's bareness and giggled with a sense of shame. When it was our turn, they sprayed us with something that smelled foul. Then they gave us a uniform to wear which made us identical. Our clean and homogenous looking group was soon back at the original office building, the one we had visited upon our return to The Hague. We had to wait a long time with the other stinky people before they called us into a big room. There were men in uniforms sitting behind desks looking at papers and there was a lot of talk back and forth with my Mom about things I did not understand, until...

They rose, took my mother by the arms and started walking her to the outside door. She was leaving without me? I ran and grabbed onto her, and it took two men to peel me off. I kicked and screamed, and could not understand why this was happening. I realized they were holding Mom, but could not understand why she was not trying to get away from those bad people. After the two men ripped me from her, I hung between them, one held my arms and the other held my legs. I still struggled to get loose as I saw Mom disappearing through a glass door and then driven off in an open car.

I was devastated. This was now the second time I was separated from Mom. The first time was when I was sent to that white place for children. This time was different. I didn't know what those terrible men were going to do to her or where they were taking her. I did not see this coming at all. Why was this happening to us? Mom had said, "The war is over and we are going home".

My heart was sinking once again as the world was so uncertain. All I could see was that Mom was gone and that was all that mattered. I wept from deep within and tried to hold on to the image of her.

FOUR

The Orphanage

Without any explanation, I was deposited in a car too, the same military-type car that carried my mother away. I hoped the people driving realized that they had made a big mistake and were bringing me back to Mom. Instead, they took me to a school, and I was handed off to a woman who told me to play with the other children. Playing was the last thing I wanted to do. I did not know what to think of this place. Was it a school or a play place?

The school building, filled with filthy children of all ages, reeked of body odor. No one told me where to go, so to get away from the smell I walked to an outside cement courtyard and sat. Some children were on swings while others were building a playhouse from bales of hay that were lying around. I simply sat there for what seemed like hours.

Soon the children were going inside but I continued to sit since I didn't know where I was supposed to go. The sun was sinking and I got cold so I moved into the playhouse that the children had made and covered myself with straw for warmth. I was softly crying for Mom, when a face suddenly peeked through the opening. It was an older boy with a kind face who asked me why I was there. I told him that I didn't know why, so he took me inside to find an adult. My stomach rumbled with hunger but I was too upset and too tired to talk about it. As a matter of fact, I did not talk at all.

A woman escorted me into a classroom filled with wooden beds. The room was dark because the children were already sleeping. Guided by the moonlight, she led me to an empty bed in the corner. It was perched alongside a window, which overlooked the courtyard. Again, I slept on a straw sack with horse blankets, but this time it was wet from pee and smelled dreadful. I laid there looking at the stars thinking if I lay very still, I would not feel the wetness or smell the awful stench. It must have helped, or I was simply exhausted because I fell asleep. The bedding was never changed; the pee just dried up and I smelled it all the time.

It smelled even worse at the place where food was served. There were so many children at meal times that all of us together created a dirty, sour, rotten, poop smell. The food was a soupy mush with unidentified stuff in it and bread that didn't have that great Canadian bread taste that I remembered. Where were those friendly Canadian soldiers? They must have gone back to their country I thought to myself. Their departure was too soon, because things were abominable here. I needed those kind, cheerful, generous soldiers now more than ever.

My time at the orphanage was a difficult one, as expected. What made it most difficult was how fast I had to adapt to it. When the war officially ended in Holland on May 5, 1945, I was beside my Mother. It was only a week or two later that I was torn from her without any explanation, and thrust into a life of unknown at the orphanage.

I was having nightmares just about every night. In one I saw Mom walking in the street, I would call out to her, but she would round the corner without hearing me. I would run to catch up to her but as I went around that corner, she was turning the next. This scene would repeat until I woke up. The same nightmare would happen with stairs. I would run as fast as I could up the stairs or would almost fly down the stairs, but I was never able to catch up with her. It always ended with me waking up in tears. My beloved doll Antje would have helped comfort me during this difficult time, but she was gone as well. I had no idea what had happened to her. I missed her, but more than that, I missed Mom very much. Every time I thought of her, I felt this deep pain inside.

I thought there must be someone who could help me find my Mom. It had to be someone important. I was only six, but I had survival experience. I knew how to hide when I heard airplanes, how to find food, and how to defend myself. I was not afraid to throw stones again if I had to. I had seen hunger, misery, death, and numerous nasty people, old and young who would not think twice about hurting me. I hoped I could find the person in charge of this place and he could help me find Mom. My search began with me exploring my immediate surroundings, which I had not done since I arrived.

There was an office at the school and I thought that was the place to go to when people came to work in the morning. I looked for the most impressive person I could find. There was a man wearing a uniform covered with badges. Even though he did not know it yet, I was convinced I had found my helper.

Every morning, I waited at the bottom of the stairs for this gentleman to arrive. When he passed me, I would say, "Can you please take me to my mother?" He never said anything back to me, but I would repeat these words every day. They were actually the only words I spoke, as I did not speak to anyone else. After many mornings repeating this ritual, someone gave me Antje. I was elated to have my coveted Antje back in my arms, but also baffled that she suddenly appeared and how they knew she was my doll. I remember thinking to myself, what other secrets does this place hold?

While wandering through the orphanage I discovered an outside door at the back of the building. Much to my surprise the handle turned and I stood in the open doorway contemplating whether to step through. I remember asking myself, where would I go, but sadly did not have an answer. I gazed at this outside world with strange eyes. It was a world that resembled and sounded like the one I remembered, but it gave me a feeling that I did not belong anymore. I didn't know why, but I was convinced that if I left this place, the people outside would know that. They would not help me, only bring me back, and I would be in trouble. I was frightened someone would notice me at the door so I softly closed it. A couple of times I reconsidered, but each time I found myself saying I would leave the next time. Unfortunately I waited too long because one day I found my exit locked.

Head lice was a big problem and all the little children's heads had to be shaved. Mom always told me I had beautiful hair. I was afraid if she saw me without it, she would be upset. Upsetting mom was absolutely the last thing I wanted to do. Thus, I was determined to avoid getting my head shaved.

When the time came for scalping, I hid in a bathroom stall until it was dark. I missed a meal but it was worth it. I was elated and so were the lice that remained living in my hair. I did not know the cut off age for head shaving, but no one ever questioned me. To my advantage, I was tall for my age. I am assuming the staff at the orphanage thought either they had my age wrong, or maybe they just didn't care. The place was not well organized. Looking back, the staff had also seen rough times, and didn't care much for their jobs.

Walking through the orphanage one day, a teenage girl suddenly called out to me. It was Annie; she not only was from my old neighborhood but also with us in Valkenburg. I was so relieved and delighted to see her. She took me upstairs to a bright, sunny hallway where the older girls bunked. From that point on, I stayed by my old friend's side. Annie and the older girls tended to me and became like family. They made sure I was well fed and gave me some warm things to wear when I was cold in the night. Life was definitely much better with them; I felt safe and quite happy. They talked about how awful the orphanage was, confirming my feeling that this was not a normal kind of life. Maybe they would see a way out. I thought they probably knew how to get to the café where I used to live. I decided I would stay with them and eventually they would get me home.

Not long after I moved in with the older girls, a woman came and brought me into a big office. Large, colorful Oriental rugs covered the office floor, and behind an enormous dark brown desk sat the important man I spoke to every morning. He asked me to come closer. As I approached the desk, the man asked me if I knew the woman who was sitting opposite him. I thought she resembled my Mom. However, I did not know who she was. The man informed me that she was my Aunt Jo and I was to go home with her. This should have made me ecstatic, but it didn't. I would much rather stay with the big girls than go with her. I was confused. I asked him every day to take me to my mother. Why did he bring me someone who just looked like her?

FIVE

Aunt Jo

As the train rumbled down the tracks, my lips remained sealed as I examined Aunt Jo with my apprehensive eyes. She was a complete stranger to me but I found her face comforting since it resembled my mother's. Anyone seeing the two together would know they were sisters. Aunt Jo was not lanky like Mom and a bit heavier. Her hair, gray like Mom's, was tucked neatly in a low bun at the nape of her neck. She lived in Amsterdam with her husband Adriaan and stepdaughter Jopie. Her simple phrase, "Here we are," jolted me from my pondering into reality. A dark green door opened and I stepped into a long dim hallway. At the end was the kitchen, where another doorway on the left led to the living room. There my Uncle and Jopie were waiting. I was nervous and scared. This was a whole new place for me and I didn't know any of these people. Uncle Adriaan had a heavy round face that looked like it could explode any moment, and a stocky body. Jopie had curly brown shoulder length hair and was a mature young woman.

Upon arriving to their home, Aunt Jo and Jopie immediately got to work on my hair, which was still infested with lice. Aunt Jo combed my hair over a newspaper and Jopie killed the lice as they fell. I was glad they were doing this. However, their derogatory comments left me feeling dejected and too dirty to touch. I was filthy, but it certainly wasn't on purpose. After the meticulous combing, they put a powder on my head that would kill the lice eggs and any lice that remained. Aunt Jo then placed a cap on my head to prevent the insects, dead or alive, from falling out all over the place. I looked abysmal, smelled terrible, and felt I was everyone's laughing stock.

Aunt Jo and Uncle Adriaan.

At the close of another pivotal day, I cried myself to sleep that first night at Aunt Jo's Amsterdam home. I was missing the older girls at the orphanage who had been so sweet to me. My tears continued each night for various reasons. My beloved Antje went missing again a few days after arriving at Aunt Jo's. I think Aunt Jo threw her away because she was filthy, and probably had lice too. I longed for my lovely little dolly and wished she was still by my side to comfort me. Antje and I had been through so much together something Aunt Jo didn't know anything about. Otherwise, I don't think she would have thrown her out. What I didn't know about Aunt Jo was that she was originally Uncle Adrian's housekeeper. After his wife died, he needed someone to take care of him and his daughter Jopie. Aunt Jo married him, but that didn't change anything except she no longer received a salary. I never witnessed much tenderness between them. I do recall a large photograph of his first wife on his desk in the corner of the living room. There were always fresh flowers next to it put there by Aunt Jo. Looking back, I wonder if Aunt Jo found her position in the family difficult or emotionally trying. Did she ever feel like the wife/mother of the household? Did she truly love Uncle Adriaan or was their marriage purely because of circumstances?

Life was arduous in Holland after the war. Food was scarce, rationed with coupons, and choices were limited. We mostly ate mashed potatoes mixed with sauerkraut, apples, or carrots and onions for dinner. Still not the stellar eater and exploring my creative side, I would construct streets with houses, lakes and rivers with my food. My fork would traverse these creations as a car or boat. Uncle Adriaan was not fond of me playing with my food and told me that food was not a toy. What else was there to play with?

There are many places from my childhood that I distinctly remember. Aunt Jo and Uncle Adrian's living room was one I can picture in detail. The dining table sat in the middle of the room underneath a large beige fabric lamp with numerous pleats and ruffles, which hung from the ceiling. I soon discovered that Aunt Gre, my Mom's other sister, made this ornate lamp. The whole family was very proud of it, including me. I was amazed that my Aunt could make something so beautiful and intricate. Behind the dining table was a cupboard that stored all the things needed to set the table. Table setting became my job. I had to know which plate, fork and knife belonged to whom because everyone had his own and they were all different from each other.

The brown wooden clock, which sat dead center on Aunt Jo and Uncle Adriaan's mantle, stands out most in my memory. My place at the table faced that clock, the clock that I would eventually learn how to tell time on. Since I had to go to bed at seven, I tried to figure out where that was on the clock and to see how much time I still had before going to sleep. Jopie told me later they pushed the clock forward when they wanted me to go to bed earlier. Sometimes there was an orange next to the clock that the four of us shared for dessert. I would stare at it throughout the entire meal. I could hardly wait to taste such a delicacy.

To the right of the living room there were glass doors that opened to the sun lounge where I slept. My room had doors that opened to a garden with beautiful white roses growing on the back wall. I loved being out there dancing like a butterfly and smelling the lovely roses. Orange nasturtiums in various shades covered the ground like a blanket and smelled just like fragrant tea to me. Summer in that garden was heaven on earth.

My shoes were more holes than shoe when I arrived at their home. The soles flapped with every step and my feet were always dirty and wet when it rained. Uncle Adriaan was a shoemaker and tried to fix my worn pair as best he could. The front room of the apartment held large shoe repair machines that would noisily run all day long. Uncle Adrian must have been a master of the trade with those machines since other shoemakers brought their costumers shoes for him to repair. One day Uncle Adrian came from the front room and gave me a pair of shoes he had made for me from scratch. They were black, big and ugly with plenty of room to grow. I did not mind, I proudly wore my new shoes and told everyone my Uncle had made them for me.

Aunt Jo certainly doted on Uncle Adriaan. So there had to be some love there or maybe it was more subservience to the male of the household. As I had stated earlier, post war life in Holland was difficult. Everything required coupons, and still it was not enough. My uncle's needs came first. He ate an egg a couple of mornings a week, either soft-boiled or raw with sugar. If I was lucky, he would leave a little egg white in the shell or I could lick the cup after he finished his raw egg. On the rare occasion there was something special to eat, he would be the one to enjoy it. I even felt, if he had asked my aunt to chew his food for him, she would have gladly done that too. Uncle Adriaan was clearly king of the house.

At the end of August when I was six and a half, Aunt Jo enrolled me in the first grade at a Christian school. My favorite part of the school day was singing the religious songs they taught us. I tried singing them in harmony and thought I was pretty good at it. Every night before going to sleep, I knelt beside my bed and sang a little song.

I go to sleep, I am tired.
I close both of my little eyes.
Lord, please watch over me this night like the nights before.

Each night after my devote tune, I would pray for my parents return. I was still oblivious to their whereabouts. I presumed Aunt Jo had no idea either and that was the reason I had to pray to God so he would help me find them. Timid and afraid, I did not ask any questions. This was a time when children were supposed to be seen and not heard. This was especially true in Uncle Adriaan's household.

Uncle Adriaan's daughter, Jopie, was dating at the time. Her boyfriend visited our home in the evenings. When my aunt and uncle were not in the living room, her boyfriend Nico dipped her backwards on his arm and planted a lengthy kiss. I witnessed their sincere affection through the glass doors when they thought I was sleeping. It made me giggle and I always hoped to see more romantic dips before I fell asleep.

Other than Jopie and Nico dip-kissing when nobody was looking, the family was stiff and proper. This was drastically different from my most recent vagabond wartime life with Mom. We often went places we were not supposed to be when searching for food. Property or rules were meaningless; we were starving and needed to survive. Later on when I was separated from Mom at the orphanage with all the other children, there was an abundance of freedom. I don't remember any rules, and quickly learned to be as anonymous as possible in order to stay away from trouble. Before I met and joined the older girls, I fended for myself. Aunt Jo had no idea how independent I had become at that orphanage.

Aunt Jo and Uncle Adriaan had rules and for a curious, young girl like me they were difficult to follow at times. For instance, I was forbidden to go to the playground by myself after school, even though I was quite capable of taking care of myself. One day I could no longer resist the fun and enticing playground. I came home sick from all the turning and swinging and was shocked that my aunt and uncle knew about my playground rendezvous. I was in trouble and never played there again. Rules were rules.

The candy store was another place of enticement and conveniently located next to the playground and of course on my route to school. They sold all kinds of delectable penny candy. What intrigued me most were those sheets of edible candy paper! Countless times I stood pressed against the candy store window and dreamed about what I would purchase if I had the money. The delicate candy paper was always first on my list. Little did I know, soon I would taste these sweet treats. Temptation can be irresistible for a small girl.

School sent home a note informing families that there would be a monthly collection for the poor, starving children of Africa. The next day Aunt Jo placed ten cents in my palm for those poor children and never missed giving me money in the months to follow. On one of those occasions, temptation got the best of me and I did not give the money to the teacher. Instead, I used it to buy the edible paper. It is called ouwel in Holland, and is similar in texture to the communion wafers used in the Catholic Church. The only difference is ouwel came in different colors and had some flavor. What I loved most was the paper effect and how it dissolved magically on my tongue. Finally, I was able to enjoy this treat. That I took food away from those poor starving children in Africa was far from my mind at that point.

My joy of tasting these forbidden candies was fleeting. How Aunt Jo found out about the candy store is once again a mystery. Clearly, crime does not pay. At school, I was punished for my bad behavior. My teacher put me in the corner of the class where everyone could see what a rotten girl I was for stealing from the poor children in Africa. I felt terrible about what I did, but what really made me angry was how my teacher went on and on about it. He even asked my classmates what they thought about my behavior. I can still see myself in that corner hating everything and everybody. I didn't look forward going home and getting another lecture about my behavior but that never came. Aunt Jo and Uncle Adriaan just asked me if I learned my lesson. Yes I did.

At the end of the school year, Aunt Jo and I boarded a train to Egmond-on-Sea where Aunt Gre and her family resided. I was excited to meet the maker of the beautiful lamp I admired every day. Aunt Gre lived in a tent on the beach with her husband and two sons for the whole summer. Lucky for me, they invited me to join them.

The tent was substantial with a little window in the back. We had simple sleeping bags made from a blanket sewn together on three sides. They were placed on top of straw bags, but unlike the ones from my past, these were sweet smelling and free of insects. There were tents on the left and right of us with families enjoying summertime. Everyone was in vacation mode and that made it

a happy place to be. Life on the beach was very simple but perfect. Now when I go camping with my Grandchildren Alexa and
Hudson for a couple of days, I think about Aunt Gre and wonder
how she did it every summer without any basic conveniences.

Aunt Gre and Uncle Ben were the happiest people I knew,
ecstatic about life and each other. Aunt Gre was younger than
Mom, less grey, and smiled a lot; something I hadn't seen much of
with Mom or Aunt Jo. With Aunt Gre anything was possible. She
could whip up a delicious meal on a small kerosene stove and had
unique ways of doling out food. I remember specifically when she
had to cut slices of bread for us. Aunt Gre held the bread under
her arm and while she cut it, we caught the slices before they fell
in the sand. Uncle Ben had a bald head, which reminded me of
a round Dutch Gouda cheese. He was always able to put a smile
on my face and loved teasing my aunt and she ate it up. Upon his
arrival after a day's work, Uncle Ben would hold Aunt Gre very
close kissing her neck and refusing to let her go. She pretended
to be embarrassed, struggling to get away and asking for our help.
Her sons and I were eager to do so, and after a lot of giggling and
laughter we all ended up falling in the sand.

Uncle Ben was head of maintenance at a hospital in Alkmaar,
a city west of the beach. He always brought us delicious goodies
when he came home to the tent. One time he brought a big pail
of slippery silver herring. Aunt Gre had to do the dirty, smelly job
of cleaning them, which was not an easy task in a tent without
running water. Indulging on as many herring as you can consume
was one of the highlights of that summer and still is. After we
finished cooking and eating, we cleaned the pots and pans with
sand in the North Sea. I had the best time there. I played, danced
and frolicked on that beautiful beach every day that summer. I
received hugs and affection, and was happy and content. Looking
back, my memories with Aunt Gre and Uncle Ben were the happiest of my childhood.

At the close of the summer and with my inevitable return

to Aunt Jo in Amsterdam, I became melancholy. I missed Aunt Gre terribly and cried the first night back in Amsterdam. Aunt Jo heard my sobs and came into my room to see what was wrong. I told her my eyes were hurting, because I didn't want to hurt Aunt Jo's feelings. Eventually, I got back into my school year routine and life in Amsterdam resumed. At least now I had my blissful summer memories to reflect on and relive.

Although so much had happened to me, I still thought about dancing all the time. There was an entryway in front of my uncle's apartment, and this became my stage. Jopie had a couple of old summer dresses that she let me use for costumes. I cut them up and made them beautiful. I danced for the children in the neighborhood and made up little plays, which were mostly stories about princesses. I assigned the little parts to other children, but I always had the leading role. I played and danced until the prince found me, because somehow, I was always lost. Each play ended the same way, the prince and princess living happily ever after. Because children were not allowed inside the house, I played outside with the neighborhood children. I always felt a little down when it was time to go home.

Aunt Jo took good care of me, but in the beginning I was not very happy. I felt no one really cared for me. Maybe they thought I was not a nice person. After all, I did use the money for the starving kids on candy for myself. Then there was Uncle Adriaan's little nephew, who was my age. He lived on a farm in the province of Brabant, and was invited to keep me company. I remember sitting under the dining table with him. I don't remember exactly what I said, but I know my words were hurtful. My uncle was napping in the inner room next to the living room. Apparently he heard enough, because before I knew it I felt a big kick under the table. I deserved it. Uncle Adriaan's nephew had a normal life, a home with a mother and father who loved him. Naturally I was jealous.

I did not allow myself to become very attached to Aunt Jo or anyone else. I felt the most comfortable with Aunt Gre after staying with her. I thought I was going to live with Aunt Jo, but was never sure. I was fooled when I was separated from Mom, it taught me not to be sure of anything.

One day out of the blue, Aunt Jo told me we were going to visit Mom. I could not belief my ears. It was over a year since I last saw her, and I was having a hard time picturing her face. We took the train to The Hague, and walked to a building that looked like a hospital. Aunt Jo and I walked through long hallways. Every time I turned the corner and thought now I see Mom there was another hallway to walk through. I was reliving my nightmares in this place. We finally stood in the doorway of my Mom's room. It was a big room with many beds and women. I recognized Mom sitting on one of the beds. I looked her over while walking to her and thought that she looked so different in this odd place, a place that I could not quite figure out. It didn't make me happy or sad seeing her, just very uncomfortable.

Mom kissed me and we talked about little things like how big I was getting and how I was doing in school. When Mom commented on how long my hair was getting, I was thrilled. I had dodged getting my head shaved because I knew how much Mom liked my hair, and now she admired it. I didn't tell her what I had to do to keep it long. Then Mom examined my hands and said, "What am I seeing? YOU BITE YOUR NAILS?" It scared me so much I never bit my nails again. The visit was short which was fine with me. The hospital was unpleasant, crowded with beds and filled with women who looked out of place. I was relieved I did not have to stay there with Mom and could go back home with Aunt Jo.

In the beginning, it seemed like Aunt Jo was not comfortable with me. This was probably because she was not accustomed to taking care of small children. That changed over time. I began to realize she cared for me and I started to love her as well. There was no hugging or much kissing, but I was used to that. Aunt Jo's hands told me that she cared. These hands washed me, combed my hair, helped me dress, gave me spoons full of cod liver oil and when I needed those hands they would hold mine. Before Aunt Jo met Uncle Adriaan, she had worked for another family where some kind of chemical had destroyed the nail beds of all her fingers. To other people, her hands must have looked terrible, but to me they were Aunt Jo's beautiful loving hands. Both my Aunt Jo and Uncle Adriaan were there at a time when I needed them most, and I am forever grateful to them.

Living with Aunt Jo was home to me and I didn't think things were ever going to change. Then one day in the spring of 1947, Aunt Jo announced we were going to my Aunt Cor's house and that Mom would also be there. Aunt Cor was one of Mom's sisters whom I had met once when she visited Aunt Jo. Aunt Cor was overweight and had short permed gray hair that reminded me of a dandelion flower that turned to seed. When she walked, it looked like she had the urge to go to the bathroom and had absolutely no patience for anything or anyone.

Apparently, Mom was no longer in the strange hospital and was now living with Aunt Cor. This visit with Mom was better, even though I still felt a distance between us. Most of the conversation between the sisters was over my head. To keep me occupied Aunt Cor let me play her piano, but only for a couple of minutes because it was all she could take. After that, she gave me a box of tiny black and white baby dolls to play with. I happily kept myself entertained with those babies while the three women were talking. It must have been a serious adult discussion because I could not understand anything.

After a meal of food that tasted way too salty, it was time for us to leave. I was happy to go back to Amsterdam with Aunt Jo. Over the next couple of months, we would visit Mom and Aunt Cor maybe two more times. Seeing Mom again made life a bit more complicated when it came to my feelings. I had become very close to Aunt Jo. At times I would ask myself if I cared for her more than I cared for Mom. It is a strange thought to have; Mom was my real mother after all. As for my Papa, I had not seen him since leaving the café and still had no idea his whereabouts. Maybe he was dead and they didn't want to tell me.

I spent another summer with my Aunt Gre on the beach, but this time I was not as happy to be there. At eight years old and just finished second grade I could understand things better. With all that was going on, an emotional roller coaster of sorts, I must have been a little depressed.

Shortly after I came back from my summer vacation with Aunt Gre, I was united with my parents.

Mom and I in front of our houseboat.

SIX

Growing Up On The IJ Canal

From Aunt Jo's house we took tramline 4 to Central Station. For a penny, an old bus could take you to the other side of the station but we walked. For Aunt Jo, a penny saved was a penny earned. From there we took the ferry across the IJ Canal to Amsterdam North. We walked for about twenty minutes along a canal until there it was, a small houseboat, my new home.

At last my parents welcomed me home. It had been so long since I last saw them, especially Papa. Things were not the same as before, my parents had become strangers to me and I didn't know how to behave with them. I didn't understand why they abandoned me and let me fend for myself. I was angry with them. Where were they when I needed them? Where was Papa when those men were pulling me off Mom? Why didn't Mom try to get me out of that hideous orphanage? I had so many unanswered questions, questions about events that still shook me to my core. I was too shy to talk about anything at that point. Because they never asked me how I felt, I thought I was not expected to talk about it. Therefore, I never got the answers to my questions.

Our first days as a family were especially uncomfortable. Once again I was in a strange place, only this time it was with parents I hardly knew. I was very upset when Aunt Jo left, I cried for her that first night. My mother heard me and asked what was wrong. It was her turn to hear that my eyes were hurting.

41

My parents were able to buy this little houseboat because someone had been considerate enough to return one of their billiard tables from the café. It was the only item returned to them after the war. The houseboat had three little compartments. The entrance was low so adults had to be careful not to hit their heads going down. There were three steps down to the sitting, eating and cooking area. On one side was a small folding table with a window above it. There were three chairs, two regular ones and my makeshift one, which was a sewing box on legs facing the window. Our sink was connected to a tank on the roof for water, and there was a coal stove for cooking that also provided heat.

The second compartment was reached through a sliding door. This simple place was where I slept. My bed was the length of the compartment and opposite was a small cabinet containing dishes and groceries. The third compartment was where my parents slept. Their bed was high up over the front part of the boat in an extension. It was the only place where you could hang clothes and store items.

The boat had no running water, bathroom facilities, or electricity, so we used oil lamps and a chamber pot. My father filled the tank on the roof with buckets of water he got from a pump up the road. The street had a long row of houseboats on one side, and factories on the other. The houseboats came in all shapes and sizes but none of them were smaller than ours. I had been in worse places in my life and didn't question this lifestyle at all.

Since I didn't feel comfortable or very close to my parents anymore, I was afraid to ask for what I needed. I waited for them to offer me things. At first, I was much like a shy polite guest. When they enrolled me in school, I knew this would be my home. There would be no more roaming around. The Apeldoorselaan where we once lived, constantly on my mind during and right after the war, turned into a distant memory. The houseboats and my new surroundings were becoming home.

Mom became friends with a woman who lived on a neighboring houseboat. I called her Aunt Abby, even though she wasn't really my aunt. She had curly brown, permed hair, and always wore bright red lipstick that would run into the little lines around her mouth. She spoke with class and sophistication, at least it seemed that way to me. I sensed that she had not always lived on a houseboat. Aunt Abby had lost her husband, but I don't know how, and don't know if it had anything to do with the war. She had a small Maltese named Rukie. I loved this little dog and considered him as much mine as hers. When my parents played cards with Aunt Abby, she would bring Rukie. Together we would sleep under the blankets. If they played cards on her boat, I would snuggle with Rukie and end up sleeping over. Aunt Abby's boat was frigid on a winter night, but she always whipped up a great breakfast when I stayed over. That surely made up for the cold night.

Aunt Abby had relatives who immigrated to Canada. They sent her magazines, and although I couldn't read English, I loved looking at the pictures. I was fascinated by the tree lined streets and big beautiful houses with porches. The families were always smiling and I could understand why. If I lived there, I would be smiling too. Then there were all those pictures of food including things I didn't even recognize. It all looked so delicious. I now understood where those Canadian soldiers who had helped us in Visselhuvelde came from. No wonder they wanted to go back home as soon as possible. Their country looked wonderful. There was a picture in one of the magazines of a strawberry short cake, and I asked Aunt Abby if I could cut it out. I had just tasted my first strawberries and had loved them so much I wanted to hang that picture over my bed.

Even though we had very little, I never felt poor. Just about everyone near us was in the same situation. We usually ate very simple, one-pot meals. I liked whatever Mom made, except kidneys and cow's udder. The udder tasted like disgusting fatty blubber and it was quite a job to get it down my throat. Mom did all the cooking on one kerosene burner. When she made rice, she put the pot under the pillows of our beds after it had been boiling for a while and there it became fluffy and stayed warm while she prepared another part of the meal. Much later, when I lived on my own, I thought that was the way to make rice and used my pillows the same way my mother did. During the winter, it was easier for her to cook, because the coal stove was on giving her cooking space. Life on the houseboat was not much different than camping on the beach with Aunt Gre, but at least there were no spiders on the beach. Just before bedtime, Mom made Papa go around the boat on a spider hunt. Papa carried his oil lamp and cleared the boat of spiders, so we wouldn't worry about them crawling over us at night.

Living like this must have been hard for my parents, but for me it was normal. I disliked some things, especially going on the chamber pot that my parents had already used. I would sit on it, afraid to feel any wetness and hold my nose. Just the thought of smelling something dirty made my stomach turn. Washing my face in the morning with the same water my Papa already used was also repulsive. The water had little white things floating in it from the soap.

We didn't have a radio for the first year on the boat and television was something I never even heard of. For entertainment Papa would tell me a story every night before going to bed. They were stories about Antje, my little dolly, and Toontje, her brother. He said that Antje missed her brother so much and that was why she left me to be with him. Even though I knew this story wasn't true, it was soothing anyway. He would tell me their little adventure and after the story was over, would tell me what the story was going to be about for the next night. It made me feel good to hear about my little dolly. I couldn't wait to hear what they were up to next. After going to bed, I heard Mom reading a book to Papa. I listened to that until I fell asleep.

Me in my woolen bathing suit.

Papa fishing behind our houseboat.

Me with Mom and Aunt Abby with Rukie on her lap.

SEVEN

Rowing With The Oars You Have

Papa started a business selling utensils to chefs. Chefs supplied their own tools in the restaurants where they worked. Papa would visit them in their kitchens with his samples. His selling territory not only included Amsterdam but other big cities throughout Holland. Since there was little money for traveling expenses, Papa hitchhiked with his heavy suitcase laden with knives and utensils.

On days when I was off from school, I would accompany him. They were like adventures to me. The hitchhiking and riding in a car made it a good day. One time in particular stands out in my memory or it very well could be a combination of a few trips with Papa. We had hitched a ride to a city. And as usual, asked the driver to let us off at the railroad station. There we rented bikes and peddled from restaurant to restaurant. I waited patiently outside while he pitched his sale, which was often a long time because Papa could talk endlessly. Peeking through those kitchen windows, I would always see him talking and laughing with the chefs. While Papa was having a jovial time selling his wares, I often wondered if he even remembered me waiting outside. I was always overjoyed when he sold something because it made my wait worthwhile. After a lunch of cheese sandwiches in a quiet park, my treat of the day was a visit to a café. Papa would order coffee and I had my favorite treat, Hero Cassis soda. It was made of elderberries and had a unique flavor.

Mom also had a part in Papa's business. She bought a sewing machine and sewed chef aprons and pastry bags for Papa to sell. When she was not sewing for Papa, she was doing piecework for a company, making bathing suits. Her trusty machine seemed to be constantly running. I remember being relieved when bathing suit season was over. With winter coming, it was now time for Mom to start knitting. She could knit so fast that you could hear the needles clicking. Things were not always as warm as she expected. She knitted me a jacket but the wind blew right through it. There is always a solution to everything and mine was putting newspapers under it. Mom had taught me how to knit. So when I got a doll from Sinterklaas, which was affordable only because it had a hole in her head, I made her a scarf with the help of Mom.

During this time, life consisted of the houseboat, the water, and the smoke that blew over us from the Amsterdam refuse incinerator. Gradually there were some improvements. We finally had a toilet and a new entry way built on the back of the boat. Now people would not clunk their heads upon their arrival to our floating home. An electric line was installed as well, even though we didn't have electrical appliances. It was merely for one light bulb, which hung over the kitchen table. My father still had to fill the water tank with buckets so the washing situation didn't change. The best improvement was the toilet; it made me feel like a normal person.

Spring had arrived, and our school had the lovely idea to offer swimming lessons before school. If you wanted to know torture, this was it. April and May are not the warmest month in Holland. I would bike to the swimming pool with my friend Martha and arrive already chilled to the bone. A quick change into our bathing suits; mine a homemade woolen one, made from left over wool in a array of colors. We then plunged into an ice-cold pool wearing a harness which was tied to a kind of fishing pole. Instructors used the pole to drag each swimmer from one end of the pool to the other. While being dragged we were instructed to move our arms and legs in the basic frog style, or breaststroke. Unfortunately, there was only one fishing pole, so when you were done you watched the others while standing on the side wet and cold. Needless to say, I learned to swim very quickly that Spring. Those swimming lessons paid off that hot summer. On the end of our street was a dock on the IJ canal and that was our private pool. It didn't bother us that there was garbage, dead fish, dead rats, and even once a dead dog floating all around.

Fortunately, I was going to stay with Aunt Gre that summer but not as long as before. Mom and I peddled from our house boat to Egmond, a trip that took us all day with just a little brake to eat our sandwiches. Mom would stay one night on the beach too and then went home on her bike. That year there was a big storm at the beach. In the middle of the night, we had to rescue all our belongings and take it into the dunes. The water came all the way to the first dune, which is called the watcher. We dragged all our things into the second dune called the dreamer. That was as far as we could go because it was covered with blackberry bushes. We all huddled under a tarp and stayed there for the rest of the night. It was a little scary but also very exciting.

In the Fall, our houseboat developed a small leak, which worsened over time. Papa opened the floor in our sitting compartment, and scooped out the water. He took a cloth with a blob of grease on it, pressed it into the hole and jammed it with a piece of wood. I was so impressed and convinced he could fix anything. The blob of grease was holding it for now, but it was just a temporary fix. Winter was approaching and the cold could make it worse. My parents hired a boat to tow us to a shipyard for repairs. Papa was in the towboat, while Mom and I sat at the table in our own houseboat. We thought this would be a lot of fun, an adventurous three-day vacation in our own home. Adventurous it was but enjoyable and vacation-like it was not. Our unseaworthy houseboat had to be towed across the rough and busy IJ canal. We rocked side to side from all the giant wakes by the passing big ships. I can

still hear the loud sound of the sliding door opening and clos-
ing, but we could not do anything about it. It was so rough we
couldn't even stand up. We hoped Papa could see how ferociously
the waves tossed us from side to side. However, it was impossible
for him to see because of the high front of our boat. Mom and
I were terrified the plug holding the leak would get loose and we
would sink. This would be even more disastrous because Mom
could not swim. Miraculously, we arrived safely at the shipyard. I
remember when we walked off the boat sick and shaky, Papa said
with a smile, "And, how was it?"

A couple of days later after the boat was fixed, Mom and I
took public transportation back to our little water spot on our
canal.

EIGHT

The Secret

I was old enough to realize and understand how terrible things were for so many people during the war. In school and from Martha and Marie's older brothers and parents I heard horrific war stories, stories that were difficult for a nine year old to hear. Horrendous events occurred because of the Germans and the Dutch group known as The Nationaal Socialistische Beweging or NSB, who cooperated with them. Daily discussions focused on the horrendous suffering of the Jewish people, the hunger winter, and the general misery and sadness caused by those rotten Krauts and NSBers. Along with everyone else, I despised the Germans and their collaborators for what they did and would sing anti-German songs with my friends all the time.

I remember coming home from school for lunch one day singing my favorite anti German song. Mom was sitting on her chair knitting. I can't recall the whole song, but the part where Mom abruptly stopped me was, "Away with the Krauts and the NSB." She glared at me angrily, "I do not want to hear any of those songs come out of your mouth again. Ever!" "Why", I asked, not understanding why my song angered her. She shouted out "BECAUSE WE WERE WITH THE NSB!"

Stunned and rendered speechless by my mother's words I plummeted into the nearest chair. Did I hear her correctly? How could this be? I was hit by a bomb! In fact, if a bomb could have hit our little houseboat and sunk us with it, I would consider it a blessing. The whole idea that I was tied to those NSBers was utterly devastating. With this news, I was part of those disgusting people who did all those appalling things, people my friends and I wanted to spit on. My head was spinning; I found this all too overwhelming to comprehend. I felt so terribly ashamed. Life had finally gotten back to a kind of normal. I had begun to feel a little closer to my parents and now this. My whole world was turned upside down again.

My mind raced. What if my friends and their families found out? I was convinced they would terminate my friendship, or even worse, ridicule and hate me. Right at that moment, I decided I would never tell anyone, ever.

Frozen in the chair that caught my shell-shocked body, I found myself staring at a thick slice of bread smothered in bacon fat and Dutch syrup. Mom had prepared this lunch while I digested her words. A lunch I was unable to eat since my stomach felt like a stone was in it. My body was shaking and I couldn't make it stop. One would think there would be more of a conversation or explanation after a huge announcement like that. I was just nine years old and clearly shaken by the news. However, it was apparent that Mom felt no need to further explain or discuss.

From her chair, Mom carried on knitting and very plainly said, "Eat your bread. You can't be late getting back to school." Exasperated by her disconnect to me and my feelings on the matter, I shouted back that I wasn't hungry and bolted outside. I couldn't look at her any longer. I felt like a big left over bomb from the war had just exploded inside of me.

Everything looked ashy and black on my walk back to school that afternoon with Martha and Marie. If they knew, if they only knew went through my head. They would never want anything to do with me. Suddenly I came to the realization I would never get married. Getting married would mean I would have to tell that person. Surely, learning about my shameful background would make him walk away. If anyone knew, they would never want anything to do with me. This was going to remain my secret forever.

Shortly after, I got very sick with a throat infection. Plagued with high fevers and a houseboat visit from the doctor, I remember asking Mom, "Am I going to die now?" Mom reassured me that I would be fine. I hoped she was right, but I was not convinced. I remember thinking this was a kind of punishment. After spending the ten cents on candy, Aunt Jo told me that God punishes you when you do bad things. I wondered if God had different levels of punishment for different levels of bad. Being an NSBer surely deserved punishment at the death level.

My secret consumed my whole being, from morning to night. I disliked myself and detested my parents. I tried my best to pretend everything was normal and nothing was wrong. At night in bed, I slowly pieced together instances from the past, which seemed "off" at the time but were now making sense. I understood why people threw stones at us when we left for Valkenburg. I would have done the same. I realized we had been on the run, going from one place to the other, because we were the enemy. We were hiding from the Dutch! How shameful was that?

When we returned to Holland after the war, no wonder no one gave my mother back our belongings; we didn't deserve them. When they peeled me off my mother to separate us, it was because she had to go to prison. I also surmised that the place they placed me was probably not an orphanage, but a prison. This also explained the absence of my father.

All these thoughts flew through my mind over and over again like a movie on repeat. Everything was different now that I had this secret. Wherever I went, it sat like a heavy block on my shoulders. I had to learn to live with it. Life went on. It would never be what it was before that fateful afternoon on the houseboat. I was changed forever.

NINE

The Big Surprise

With each passing birthday or around the holidays, I always asked my parents for dance classes. Their response remained the same, I had to wait. However, this year I had the feeling things might change. My Saint Nicholas celebration started out with me receiving a little basket filled with marzipan fruit and a real banana on top. I had only tasted a couple of bananas in my life. To get the most out of this delicacy, I savored each bite, taking a half hour to consume it. My next gift was a little brown suitcase made of pressed cardboard. I was ecstatic, inside was what I had wanted for so long. This was my future. I sat admiring the pair of black leather ballet shoes. It didn't matter that they were much too big. I knew they had to last. Beside my most prized possession was a note stating I could begin ballet lessons when I turned eleven. My dream was finally coming true!

Mom had bought my shoes in a little shop in Amsterdam called Mignon. Mignon was a one-man operation where ballet and theatre shoes were made and sold. He later made my first black leather toe shoes. The store reminded me very much of the store in the famous dance movie *The Red Shoes*. The tiny little store was hidden in a narrow dark street in the old part of Amsterdam. When you walked in there you felt you entered the world of magic and make believe with all kinds of strange footwear, boots and ballet shoes. It mirrored the atmosphere of the store in the film except of course, it did not contain the red ballet toe shoes. The owner had informed my mother about a Russian dance teacher named Sonia Gaskell. To his knowledge she had the best ballet school in Holland. His own daughter took classes with her so my mother thought she must be reputable. Mom met with Mrs. Gaskell to see if it was financially possible. When she was told that it was six guilders a month for one class each week, she signed me up.

Sonia Gaskell lived in the Zomerdijkstraat 26 on the top floor of a building that housed mostly artists. The bottom floor was hers as well, and that served as her dance studio. My first lesson was Saturday afternoon at two. I couldn't wait! Mom prepared hot water and I went in the tub that was used for washing laundry and me. I had a bath once a week on Saturday, so I went to class nice and clean. We walked with the little brown suitcase to the ferry that crossed the IJ. Once off the ferry, we took the little bus around the railroad station like we always did, and from there took tram 25 to Amsterdam South. I anxiously asked my Mom at every stop, "Is it here?" In actuality it is a rather long trip, but that day it seemed like a trip with no end.

We arrived much too early. Once through the front door, we stood in a small hallway where we were welcomed with beautiful music. I looked to my right where the music was coming from and saw a couple dancing together. Entranced by the couple's flowed movements, they seemed weightless. I was completely spellbound. I had never seen anything so beautiful. Their dancing was so much better than the rhythmic dancing I learned years ago at the café on the Apeldoornselaan. One of the dancers was Hans van Manen. Years later Hans told me that he remembers me, tall and skinny staring at them from the hallway that afternoon.

A woman named Pop approached me and introduced herself as my teacher. She told me where I could change my clothes and instructed my mother to return later to pick me up. I quickly changed into my little black gym pants and T-shirt, and then proudly put my black ballet shoes on my white socked feet. I already tried on my ballet shoes about a hundred times, but this time it was for real! There were other girls in the dressing room who seemed to know each other. They looked me over, but didn't say anything. Too shy to say anything to them, I excitedly made my way back to the hallway, hoping to see more dancing.

Pop called us all in. It was time for my class. Eager with anticipation and goose bumps prickled my arms as I stepped into this huge, magical place. My teacher, Maria "Pop" Huisman was a beautiful blonde woman. She asked us to grasp the ballet barre and stand in first position. This was the first day of a future I never could have imagined. At that moment standing at the barre, I forgot about my secret, the houseboat, and my life across the waters of the IJ canal. I was in a totally different world, a world I never knew existed. It felt as if I had taken a powerful drug that gave me a high. I loved everything Pop taught me that day and did not want class to end. From the moment my mother picked me up, I chatted incessantly about every detail of class and how wonderful it all was.

The week in between my classes seemed endless and meaningless. Dancing was all I wanted to do. My time at the studio felt magical and provided a much-needed reprieve from my secret. Not only did I treasure the atmosphere of the dance studio but also the smell a combination of sweat, fruit, resin and perfume. This place appealed to all my senses and I was thrilled to be a part of it.

After a couple of Saturdays, a woman came in to observe our class. She looked regal and carried herself with eloquence. I thought this must be the woman I heard the girls talk about in the dressing room. I remember distinctly, we were at the barre doing our exercises and when she observed me, she began laughing. The queenly observer spoke to my teacher and pointed in my direction, then they both began to chuckle. Was I doing something terribly wrong, so wrong in fact that it was laughable? I worked even harder to perfect all my positions and exercises while feeling very, very uncomfortable. After class, the woman called me over and asked me to point my feet. I was flooded with relief, what I thought was ridicule was pure admiration from Sonia Gaskell. I realized that no one could point their feet as I could because of my natural high instep.

Mevrouw Gaskell teaching class. Gaby is third from the left, Rudi in fourth and I am on the far right.

Sonia Gaskell, the director of the school, was Jewish and was born in the Ukraine where she got her early ballet training. She had escaped to then-Palestine, and after living and working in a kibbutz for some time, she moved to Paris. She continued her ballet training there and did some performing together with another dancer. Mrs. Gaskell met a Dutch architect in Paris and later moved to Amsterdam where they married in 1939 a week after I was born. Sadly, her husband passed away some years later. Mrs. Gaskell was a driven woman, and I don't say that mildly. She exuded elegance and dressed impeccably in flowing skirts, dresses, or very wide bottom pants, and always wore high heels even when she was teaching us. One thing I remember of Mrs. Gaskell was her wonderful perfume scent, I absolutely loved it. I have searched my whole life for that scent, but have never been able to find it.

Mrs. Gaskell taught the class after mine for older and more advanced students. After some weeks, I asked her if I could stay and watch. She not only said yes, she let me dance in the advanced class. Five future colleagues, Rudi van Dantzig, Willy de la Bije, Gaby Abbink, Janine Gaffel and Mabel Alter also attended these classes. As I had wished, I was dancing most of my Saturday afternoon and savored every moment.

Sonia Gaskell, or Mevrouw which means Misses in Dutch, as every one called her occasionally asked me to sit with her when she thought I was tired. The way she was fussing over me gave Rudi van Dantzig the idea that I was a relative of hers. She would talk sweetly to me and I soaked up all the attention. To be able to sit so closely to a woman I admired so much and who smelled so lovely was an absolute dream. I never smelled perfume before I met Mevrouw, and didn't even know of its existence. I became more aware of scents and began searching for things that smelled as good as perfume. The fresh citrus scent of a bright orange tangerine I had gotten came close in comparison. I decided that I was going to make my own fragrance. I squeezed the oil out of the porous skin, added a little water and dabbed it on my skin. Much to my dismay, it was an unsuccessful attempt at perfume making. My new business went down the drain as quickly as it started.

When I began dance classes it cost six guilders a month, but after a while, Pop told me it had increased to ten. I knew it was already expensive for my parents, so I was nervous to inform them of the increase. My bike ride home that Saturday was very emotional. The possibility of my parents saying no was killing me. I came home in tears and blurted out the problem, but Papa calmed me down and reassured me that they could pay the new cost but that it was all they could afford. If the price increased again, I would have to stop taking classes. Thankfully, I never had to deal with another increase again.

During this time, I received a weekly allowance of twenty-five cents, which allowed me some simple childhood freedoms. I got my allowance on Sunday and only if I said, "Papa it is Sunday." If I would forget to say it, which happened only once, I didn't get it. Some students from the ballet school would go to Joko, the ice cream shop, after class. I loved being around those dancers and would eagerly join them if I had enough money. Not only did I enjoy being in the same company as those dancers but I loved ice cream. If I had money left over on the end of the week, I would bring it to the bank. I even had my own bankbook! No one in the bank looked surprised when I came in with my ten cents deposit, because many children did that. I loved banking and seeing the amount in my book grow. At a young age I learned the value of saving for the future, an invaluable life lesson.

Friendships with fellow dancers began to form and I found myself becoming close with two girls who were my age, Janine and Gaby. Rudi and I had sometimes little giggles after class when we did some stretching together which formed a bond between us. And then there was Willy. I looked up to her because of her incredible dancing ability. I got to know her better because some-times we rode the tram to the train station together after class. She was very motherly with me, always sharing whatever she had. On one occasion she even gave me a raison bun with cheese. I had never eaten such a delicacy and thought she must be very rich.

Every so often, Papa gave me extra money so I could join my neighborhood friends for a Sunday at the movies. Lots of push-ing and shoving went on to get tickets. Nobody ever heard of standing nicely in a line, including me. It was an absolute free for all for about two hundred kids. My friends assigned me the job of getting the tickets because I was the tallest. Typically, children got trampled in this ticket frenzy, something my friends were scared of but it didn't scare me at all. In the past I had been in similar situations. Like meal times in that school prison where I had to stand my ground. All of the hassle was definitely worth it because I loved watching Charlie Chaplin or Laurel and Hardy films. They gave me a lot of much needed laughter.

TEN

❦

The Red Shoes

After a while, everyone in my school knew I was taking ballet lessons, including the gym teacher. She was trying to create a dance for the girls in my class to Johan Strauss's "The Blue Danube" to be performed for a parents evening. The teacher had a difficult time choreographing the dance, she constantly asked for my help. I was filled with pride that my teacher thought I was able enough to assist her. The girls saw her struggle and gave her a hard time, which, didn't help. Eventually the teacher gave up all together and said to me, "You do it." This was fine with me. I made myself the star in the dance and had everyone else dance around me. My mother sewed skirts from some blue crispy paper with miniature pink rosettes on them. I thought we looked and danced beautifully in our white socks. The reason for the socks was because no one else owned ballet shoes in my class. You could only get them specially made to order from that little store in the heart of Amsterdam.

After our performance, a student's mother approached me and asked if I would like to see a dance film at her house. Of course, I said yes. The film was a British movie about a ballet dancer called, *The Red Shoes*. After watching it, I was so enthralled I could hardly sleep that night. The scenes of the movie went through my head over and over again, especially the dancing. The ballerina Moira Shearer impressed me so much; I could not get her of my mind and wished I could dance just like her. The somber ending of the film stuck with me, and would bring tears to my eyes just thinking about it. The mother who so kindly introduced me to *The Red Shoes* gave me a little ballerina pin when I went home. I had so much fun with that plastic pin. From whatever thin material left over from Mom's sewing, I would made tiny tutus for the little ballerina. That special pin marked a very memorable experience.

My school in Amsterdam North went only to the sixth grade. After that, I attended a school in the center of Amsterdam, which was quite a distance from our houseboat, thus not allowing me to have lunches at home. Janine Gaffel, my friend from my ballet class went to the same school. Her mom said that it would be okay to come to her house for lunch. Janine and her mother lived in a large apartment in one of the best neighborhoods in Amsterdam. Janine's father was a musician who played in the Concertgebouw Orchestra, one of the best orchestras in the world. Their life was very different from mine. Janine's big round dining table had a lazy Susan with about five or six Hero jam jars on it, real butter, cheese and cold cuts of all kinds. At home, we had one no-name jam jar. This jar had only looked at fruit, but in actuality had none in it. Butter was such a delicacy in my household I would ask for it for my birthday or we would have it on other special occasions like Easter. If I was lucky to get it, it would be half a pack, and forget cold cuts all together. I was growing fast and was hungry all the time. I never felt full. All that delicious food sitting in front of me at Janine's house was hard to resist. It took all my willpower not to behave like a little overeating piggy.

Janine and I loved creating dances and took advantage of any opportunity to do so. Mevrouw was kind enough to let me borrow a tutu for my parents evening performances. At the start of my dancing on one of those evenings Papa told me he overheard someone saying, "Wait until you see her. This girl can dance!" I knew this made Papa proud of me. Which in turn made me swell with pride. I was living my dream, loving it and being recognized for it.

Janine, Rudi and I in the studio. I was thirteen
at the time this photo was taken.

Dance was constantly on my mind. If I could partake in it
every day in some form, I would be in utter bliss. The government arranged outings for schoolchildren. I wished these outings would be for ballet or musical film viewings, but no such
luck. Since I was not very social with children I didn't know well,
these outings were not very comfortable for me. I remember not
speaking a word to anyone for the whole day. These outings involved a busload of loud children who smelled, including me. We
visited a playground outside of Amsterdam where we ate lunch
and stayed the remainder of the afternoon. After all the fun of
swinging and turning, we were loaded on the bus again. The only
difference from the morning was that we all smelled much worse
now. To make matters more foul smelling was that some children
would get sick in the bus. I already learned my lesson not to swing
around too much at the playground near Aunt Jo's house, but

apparently, these trips had been their lesson. Filthy children and the stench of vomit were neither healthy nor remotely enjoyable.

The government had arranged special three-day overnight trips. Families who lived in the country volunteered to host city children. Three girls in my school were close to each other. I liked them and longed to become part of their group. I was excited to find out we would all be attending the same three-day countryside outing together. They had other ideas; their fun was making my life miserable. Beginning with our shopping trip to the store with our hostess to purchase food for the weekend, the girls made fun of whatever I thought was good. Throughout the trip, they would giggle at anything I said and whisper behind my back. I think bullying was alive and well then too. It was a miserable experience and the exact opposite of my expectations of making new friends. I was so happy when it was over.

I didn't understand their behavior then, but I think I do now. I believe the girls acted this way because they were jealous, my dancing had brought me a lot of attention at school.

ELEVEN

A Little Crush

On Wednesday and Saturday, school was a half-day schedule and I was taking ballet classes on both those days now. Not only did I attend my dance class but all the other classes on those days as well. Mevrouw had a small exclusive company called Ballet Recital. They had their own schedule in the mornings so we, the afternoon students didn't run into them very often at the studio. The only time we did see them was during their performances. Maria (Pop) Huisman, my first ballet teacher was one of the dancers performing. I idolized those dancers especially Marianna Hilarides. She was the ballerina I had seen dancing with Hans van Manen when I first set foot in this magical place called the ballet studio.

An official teenage girl, I was thirteen now and had my first "crush" on one of the dancers from the company. His name was Jaap Flier, and was the most beautiful boy I had ever seen. I was not alone in my admiration, many girls including Janine was as enamored with Jaap. He was eighteen then, and the best male dancer in Holland. My crush was not just because of his looks but also his incredible dancing talent. Jaap lived a floor above Janine's apartment and was a good friend of her family. Since I had lunch with Janine every day, I was lucky enough to see him often. Just to be in the same airspace with him was enough to make me happy. The most embarrassing thing I did was drawing so called modern art pictures to give him. They were a bunch of shapes and lines.

What was I thinking? I hope he doesn't remember that. The high-light was the day that he made dance pictures with Janine and me on the roof of their apartment building. Even if it was just for a picture, it was the first partnering I did, and to top it off it was with this dancer of all dancers, Jaap Flier. I was thrilled with his attention but as these young crushes normally do, it eventually dissipated. Respect and admiration did remain for Jaap, however.

Jaap and I on the roof of Janine's apartment building.

My parents didn't see much of me since I was in the ballet studio all the time. They had no idea what my life was like there. One time Papa came to the studio to pick me up on his bicycle because mine was broken. He looked so out of place since I was not used to seeing him at the studio. Papa chatted with Mevrouw and she smiled and laughed in response. Wow, she thought Papa was funny! I distinctly remember my Papa having a very large and embarrassing grease spot on the back of his raincoat. I prayed, as any teenage girl would in my situation, that Mevrouw would not notice it. Papa must have asked her how I was doing, something my parents occasionally asked me as well. My answer to them was always the same, "Fine." I hoped my beloved teacher's response was a positive one. On our bike ride home I asked my father what they were laughing about. She had said that I could be very funny when I clowned around with Rudi van Dantzig. My father answered Mevrouw with a Dutch expression meaning, so father so daughter. She had never heard that Dutch expression and thought it was funny.

Some of my extended family did not approve of my dancing. During a visit to Heilo with my parents, I enthusiastically told Aunt Cor about my dancing and love for ballet. Shocked by her reaction to my exiting news, Aunt Cor said she could not believe my parents allowed such a hobby. A heated discussion followed between her and my parents. I heard her say to Mom, "Didn't you do enough to give the family a bad name?" That statement sent a shiver through me because it showed how everyone in the family looked at us former NSBers, with shame and disgust. They were right and that was what hurt me so much. I tried my best to bury that secret but every little thing that had anything to do with it, in one way or another made me shiver. That hurtful ugly statement came out of Aunt Cor's mouth because from her viewpoint dancing was not something a proper girl should do. Thankfully, my parents did not agree with her. If they did they would have taken my happiness away. In that case, I do not think I would be sitting here writing this book. Dancing was the only way I could cope with my horrible, shameful secret. Without it, I don't know what would have happened to me.

The studio quickly became my second home, a place where I was the happiest and where everyone made me feel comfortable. Especially now that Willy and Rudi had become part of

Mevrouw's company too. During short school vacations, I would go to the studio in the morning and stay there all day either watching the company rehearsals or joining in their classes. These classes were more difficult and challenging for me but I always tried my best. I admired these people, not only because they were such good dancers, but also because they always treated me with kindness and respect.

I had two lives. The primitive life on the houseboat that no one in the studio knew anything about, and the worldly life of the ballet studio. The world of dancing was what I wanted to be part of mostly. I am sure that if the dancers knew I was an NSBer, it would be the end of everything I loved. Thus, I became very good at suppressing those thoughts while I was in the studio with my fellow dancers. Although I was extremely grateful for my dance classes and the little extras my parents gave me, I still resented their choice and did not see them as good people. Harsh to say about your own parents but that is how I felt. I longed to be "normal" like everyone else but knew that would never be possible. This secret would be mine forever. I had two choices: suppress it and make a life for myself or let it destroy me slowly.

TWELVE

Singel

During my fourteenth year, Papa met a man named Harry who was in the same line of work selling chef utensils. Since Harry had many contacts, which would eliminate the middleman and result in more profit for Papa, they decided to go into business together.

Our lives merged with Harry's even more when we moved into the third floor of the house he shared with his wife, Rie, on the Singel canal in Amsterdam centrum. Our houseboat, home for the past six years, was now something of the past. I was happy to leave it behind because I always wondered where this little boat had come from. Since the houseboat was named Emanuel, I hoped it was not originally owned by a Jewish family who used it as a little weekend getaway before the war. Thus, I always felt the houseboat was a tie to our secret. Severing this tie and moving to the house on the Singel was liberating.

The Singel was an improvement from the houseboat, although nothing luxurious. The only heat radiated from the coal stove in the living room. There was no hot water and we had to go down two floors to the toilet, which was at the end of a long hallway. The toilet was next to Harry and Rie's kitchen. It also had a shower, which we could use occasionally. Mom and Rie became good friends. Rie was a tall, robust looking woman who overshadowed her smaller, thinner husband. She worked at a dress shop as a sales clerk and had coffee with Mom every morning before going to work. Papa and Harry also hit it off and things seemed to go well with the business. However, Mom soon learned that Harry and Rie's marriage was not very smooth and easy. Harry threatened suicide if Rie left him and would occasionally leave his wife for a couple of days. She would do the same by running and staying with her mother. Whoever stayed home, cried on Mom's shoulder, but when they came home again everything seemed fine.

One evening I went to a concert in the Amsterdam Concertgebouw with some of my dancer friends. When I returned home, there were police officers at the house. With my heart caught in my throat, the police informed me that there had been an accident. Bolting into the house, I immediately saw Papa who was busy talking with the police. Taking the stairs by twos, I found Mom safe upstairs. After calming down, Mom told me what had happened. Apparently, Harry had gone into the kitchen, removed the gas hose from the stove and placed it in his mouth. To make sure the hose would not fall out of his mouth, he tied gauze bandages around his head, and turned the gas on. Mom found him after smelling the gas upstairs and called the police, but it was too late. I was relieved to be out of the house and not witness this gruesome scene. Harry was gone, but he left a wake of trouble for my parents and Rie. He had been in charge of paying the bills for the inventory to his business contacts. Papa had trusted him to do so, but Harry never actually paid the bills. Apparently, he saw no other way out of the financial problem he had created and cowardly dealt with it. It took my parents years to pay off everything. Merging lives with Harry seemed profitable at first but certainly did not end that way. On the bright side, it got us out of the houseboat and Rie and her new husband Frits became the closest friends of my family for the rest of their lives.

THIRTEEN

Ants

I n the spring of 1953, Mevrouw was producing a new ballet called *The Spider's Banquet*. It was a story about insects in which she had four spots available to dancers from her school to dance the role of Ants. Mevrouw selected me as one of the Ants. At fourteen Mevrouw thought I was talented enough to dance with the adult dancers. I was ecstatic. The other "Ants" as we were now called by everyone in the company were my three best friends; Gaby, Janine and Mable. The four of us took classes together for the past four years, we were all about the same age, and if you saw one Ant you didn't have to look far to see the others.

Our first rehearsal is still a vivid memory with Mevrouw explaining and demonstrating what to do. At the start we stood in a line with each hand next to our forehead to make it look like an ant antennae. We appeared on stage with tiny walking steps on toe shoes. The next ballet steps incorporated picking up leafs, and it made me feel that we really looked and behaved like ants with what Mevrouw made us do.

I loved rehearsing the ballet. The music by Albert Roussel was inspiring to me, and the story was magical. Loeki van Oven, one of the older dancers in the company, was a convincing spider who kills the beautiful dragonfly, danced by our prima ballerina Marianna Hilarides. The grasshoppers, with the help of the caterpillars, then kill the spider. At the end of the ballet, everyone carries the dead dragonfly off the stage in a sad procession. I became totally immersed in the story and many times my eyes would be brimming with tears as the curtain closed.

Finally, on June 1st, 1953 at the Stadsschouwburg in Amsterdam I had my first performance. I couldn't believe I was going to dance in this biggest and most important performance theater in Amsterdam. Naturally, I was nervous and worried things would go wrong. Not because the hundreds of people in the audience, that did not faze me. What was forefront in my mind for that first performance was showing Mevrouw how well I could dance. I wanted her to be proud of me.

We wore black tights and black body suits painted to look like ants, with little antennas on our ballerina heads and black leather Minnon store toe shoes. At that time, there was a so-called ballerina hairdo. Hair parted in the middle, down over the ears and gathered at the nape of the neck in a low bun. This all had to be covered with a hairnet. I thought it would look so much better without one and refused to wear the hairnet. The Ants and older dancers tried but were not able to convince me. Mevrouw had to be called. After telling me in her sweetest voice that my hair was as fine as hers and that she always had worn a hairnet, I gave in. I guess I was headstrong in some ways.

When the performance began, I was ready and excited. Everything went smoothly. Mevrouw gave the four Ants flowers with a personal note after the performance. My parents came to see me too, and said they liked it. I was ecstatic. The Company paid us the large sum of ten guilders for every performance. If the performance was outside of Amsterdam, we got fifty cents for every hour away from home to buy food. That was half the money the older dancers got. I guess Mevrouw didn't think we needed to eat as much as they did.

My second family, the members of my dance studio, had become such an integral part of my life. I loved and admired each of them, especially Mevrouw. She was a highly intelligent person, well-educated and very strong willed. Her strong will was very beneficial to dance in Holland but was the reason that made her lose us years later. Growing up I listened intensely to what Mevrouw had to say. She gave me the perspective that the world was much bigger than the little houseboat I had been living in. She was fluent in many languages and well-read in all of them. I wanted to be close to this worldly person and learn as much as I could from her. As you know, I even wanted to smell like her.

If traveling with the company was not exciting enough, exploring the nooks and crannies of all the different theaters was even better. This became the "Ants" favorite activity. Attics were always nice and scary, and the theaters tended to have lots of dark places to play hide-and-seek. We might have been a nuisance to everyone else but we enjoyed our fun and games.

In one theater, we were playing hide and seek in the stage area. I crawled and followed Mable as she disappeared through a very low curtain. I opened it to go through it too, and found myself looking into a deep dark hole. It was the orchestra pit. I called out her name but Mable didn't respond. In a panic, the rest of us "Ants" raced off to tell Mevrouw, who sent the stage manager to look for Mable who was not in the orchestra pit. We finally found the fallen "Ant" in our dressing room, all out of sorts. It is still a mystery how she got out of that hole. The Theater Director called a doctor to look Mabel over and after checking on her, the doctor told Mevrouw that Mabel was fine. Mevrouw always had her lipstick handy for a quick touchup. There she was standing in front of the doctor putting lipstick on while saying to him in her unique accent voice, "Those Ants! You can't take them anywhere." I will never forget the man's face and wonder what must have gone through his head.

Occasionally Mevrouw would travel to New York or Paris. Places I knew about, but could not imagine ever going to myself. Upon her departure, she always looked like a million dollars, clad in the latest fashions as if she had just walked off a page of Vogue. Rudi and I could not stop staring at her. He would say,

"She looks like a woman of the world." Those trips were mostly
to visit her family, but also to connect with famous ballet teachers
and company directors. What escaped me at that time was talk
that she might not return. I was too young to know the politics
of the Dutch ballet world, and I am glad of my naivety. Mevrouw
was my idle, if she had not returned; it would have been devastating for me. In the end, it all worked out. The government decided
to subsidize a new, bigger dance company called *The Netherlands
Ballet*, with Mevrouw as director.

FOURTEEN

The Netherlands Ballet

When *The Netherlands Ballet* became reality, the four of us Ants had to audition to get in. This came as a surprise to me since we were already part of Mevrouw's little company.

The audition was held in May of 1954 at The Stadsschouwburg in Amsterdam. I retrieved my number and then wandered back stage feeling lost. Much to my surprise, I saw Rudi with a number as well which comforted me. None of us was guaranteed a position. Besides the Ants and Rudi, there were many other dancers from all over the Netherlands eager to become part of the new company. The audition was held on the stage, with the judges sitting below in the dark auditorium. We heard Mevrouw's voice, a voice none of us could mistake penetrating the darkness, confirming her presence. My head flooded with questions, concerns and anxiety. Was she looking for better dancers? Was she going to get rid of me this way? I thought she liked me, and now suddenly I had become just a number.

After a couple of nerve-wracking days, the results were in and a flood of relief spread over me; all five of us were accepted! In addition to our five, twelve additional girl dancers came together to form the corps de ballet of this new company.

As summer came to a close rehearsal began for the classic ballet *Les Sylphides*. It was taught to us by John Tarras, a famous choreographer who also worked with George Balanchine. In this

76

ballet everyone wears long white tutus with a circle of white flowers in their hair. I was in heaven. This was the most beautiful
ballet I ever imagined myself dancing. I was the tallest female
dancer in the company, which at that point sometimes made me
uncomfortable. As a corps de ballet dancer, you stand often in a
line together. Glancing at our reflection in the mirror, I looked
like a tall building amongst small row houses. How grateful I was
for our long tutus because I could discreetly shorten myself by
hiding a bent knee. This made me feel better. I was also very thin
and thought it was clever to wear two layers of tights when a long
tutu did not cover my legs. In her sweetest voice, Mevrouw would
call me, "Little piece of stick." It was her pet name for me. I know
it is not proper English, but that is what Mevrouw would call me.
She didn't always speak proper Dutch.

Mr. Tarras not only choreographed and taught us the ballets
he also exposed us to the English language at a level we were not
accustomed to. I had English in school but hearing it from this
impressive man who only spoke English, it sounded like Chinese
to me and nothing like what I had learned. Rehearsing his ballet
started out with a problem. The corps de ballet girls had to run
up in a circle, and the first girl did it wrong each time. That must
have made him a little cranky but he didn't show it at first. The
ballet contained an awkward part that I called a "knitting piece,"
a term I used if an uncomfortable set of steps made no sense.
Everyone was already nervous after the first girl's mishap, and
then we had trouble with this "knitting piece." My gangly body
stuck out and Mr. Tarras kept picking on me. The harder I tried,
the more mistakes I made. There are some people who seem to
enjoy making others uncomfortable. To me Mr. Tarras was one
of them.

The Netherlands Ballet was officially born with our first performance on October 6, 1954. I was fifteen years old. All the
classes and rehearsals with this bigger company were still in the
Zomerdijk Straat studio, the same place where I had my first class.

My studio was renowned. Audrey Hepburn had ballet training from Mevrouw for a while as well, though not at the same time as me. The Dutch opening of her film *Roman Holiday* was in the Tuschinski movie theater in Amsterdam. Because of her connection with Mevrouw, we danced the first part of *Les Sylphides* for her before the movie premiered. Afterwards we met Audrey on the stage for a meet and greet. I was much too shy to say a word to her but was thrilled to be so close to a famous movie star. Some dancer friends and I just stood close together and behaved like star struck teenagers. My teen years were certainly broadening my horizons, who would have thought a girl like me would be dancing on famous stages and meeting movie stars.

Like most teenagers, friendships were important to me. I had my close girlfriends, The Ants, but there was also someone very dear to me during these years. Rudi van Dantzig and I became friends when I first started participating in the more advanced Saturday afternoon classes. Rudi was blond, tall and skinny like me, with the palest, big blue innocent eyes you can imagine. Rudi and the Ants had good times together, but I had an especially close bond with him from the beginning. We shared the same humor and could talk about anything. Over the years he would give me things to read that he thought were important to know. He recommended Dutch authors, like Anna Blaman and Harry Mulisch, but also Russians like Tolstoy and Dostoevsky. Later in life, Rudi became a well-known author in Holland.

Rudi was obsessed with Russia and so was I. Ballet is important in the Russian culture, which I came to know because of him. We went to many Russian movies together seeing the Bolshoi Ballet with Ulanova. For him there was more to Russia than just ballet. He and his parents were communists, and although I was not, I agreed with some of the things they stood for. We spent a lot of time together, going to museums, making cheap dinners of potatoes with raw chickaree and bacon when we lived on our own, and taking walks. He was the older brother I always wanted but never had. Someone I could look up to and who would stand up for me. Rudi was my brother and mentor.

I learned so much in those years as an artist, a word I despise, but also as a person. Overall, I was a little bruised by the war and did not think highly of myself because of my secret. Throughout my adolescent years, my perception about the secret did not waver. I still thought about it often but used dancing as a method of pushing away my negative thoughts. If I was dancing I was not thinking about my past or present problems, instead I was creating the atmosphere of the part I was dancing and savoring every part of it.

I often think if I could dance this book, I would do a better job with it. One can make a point in dance so clearly, for me that is easier to do than with words. Dancing was something I was comfortable with. Everyone could see that I had nothing to hide during those moments.

Although I lacked in monetary means which is probably true for most dancers, I was bountiful with the incredible richness of the people that surrounded me. These were intelligent people of all ages from various parts of the world. As a young teenager, they all played a part in my upbringing and education. Through my ballet training, I learned about life, traveled and had so many incredible experiences. All things that were above and beyond what I received in school. Dance made me the person I am today.

FIFTEEN

———— ⊰⊱ ————

Night Island

A teacher-student relationship that is symbiotic in learning will thrive; students gain a deeper understanding of subject matter and teachers learn more about their student's talents and personalities. Mevrouw had this philosophy since she gave some of her dancers the opportunity to choreograph their own work in what she called experimental programs. Rudi, known for choreographing humorous dances for our studio parties, was asked by Mevrouw to make something light and funny for this experimental program. He decided to go the opposite route making a ballet that was psychologically deep. The ballet is about a person's internal struggle trying to escape an inner dark demon. Rudi asked me to dance this with him. He would dance the main character and I would portray the dominating inner demon. In the ballet, the main character tries to envision the ultimate idealistic form of self, which was visualized by two other dancers. The main character is unable to break out of the powerful grip of his dark side. The ballet ends where it started and the person continues to struggle with the dilemma. Rudi decided to call the ballet *Night Island*. I never asked him why because I thought I understood. Every person is an island onto themselves, and for this character, it is a dark, scary and painful place from which there is no escape.

Ironically, I was given the part of the ballet that embodied the secret I had been struggling with for years. I thought to myself, how was this possible, was this a crazy scary coincidence? This secret was buried within me for seven years now. I felt this part was made for me since I could definitely embody what I had been feeling and put it into dance. Rudi did not know my secret and if I could help it, never would. He on the other hand had his own demons and wrote about them years later in a book called, *For a Lost Soldier*, which became a big bestseller in Holland.

To find music for this new ballet, we bicycled to a record store and went into a small listening room with potential pieces. We got very excited about a piece called *Six Epigraphs Antiques* (orchestrated) by Debussy. It was absolutely perfect for Rudi's *Night Island*. Excitement filled us to the point we could not sit still, we immediately started dancing and experimenting with some of the moves in that tiny listening room. Enthusiastic and eager to continue working on the ballet, Rudi and I flew out of the music store and hopped on our bikes. To this day, this memory is so vivid. I am riding my bike behind Rudi, racing back to the studio, with him holding our great find under his arm. Once back at the studio, we experimented with all kinds of unusual lifts. At times I felt I was more upside down than on my feet. Some of the lifts only worked with our bodies, especially one where my uncommon feet fit just right under his chin. Rudi always said that we choreographed parts one and four together and they were tailor made for us. Rudi set the ballet for other dancers later on at the National Ballet, but told me that he had to change some of the lifts to make it work for them.

Rudi and I were a great team, our enthusiasm poured into our work and in no time we completed the first part of the choreography. Mevrouw asked numerous times to see what we were working on, but Rudi explained it was not yet ready for showing. Since it was Rudi's first attempt at choreography, I think Mevrouw was afraid it would not be good enough to put on the program. We only worked on it when no one was around, typically in the late afternoons and evenings. Time slots that the older more established participants did not want. For five weeks, we worked until very late in the evening and loved every minute of it. For me dancing became like the bread those Canadians gave me after the war, manna from heaven. We were enthusiastic about how it was turning out, but also very nervous of Mevrouw's opinion.

Rudi and I in studio rehearsal for *Night Island.*

Once the opening portion of *"Night Island"* was completely clean, it was time to show Mevrouw. Our nerves were high but by now, I was more confident. Rudi on the other hand kept anxiously questioning, "What if she doesn't like it?" Mevrouw's opinion meant everything to us. It would be totally devastating if she was disappointed.

To our relief, Mevrouw loved it! She begged to see more but could not since parts two and three were not completely finished.

Part four was still a blank slate, so she had to wait. When members of the American Ballet Theater visited the studio while they were performing in Holland, Mevrouw proudly showed the first part of Rudi's work to them. It was an honor to perform for them and the fact that they liked it made me feel like I was walking on air. My unusual feet also got a lot of attention from them. Because of my very high instep, I can point them extremely well and that gives a nice visual line of the leg in ballet. Mevrouw always made me show of my feet to anyone who came to the studio and so did Rudi for many years. I finally told him to stop doing it because it became embarrassing to me.

With all four parts of the ballet complete and the company's support and approval, the only worry that lay ahead was what the audience would think. This performance was a major experience for me and quite possibly a turning point in my dance career. At sixteen years of age I had only danced in the corps de ballet, standing in lines with bent knees whenever possible. *Night Island* would showcase my true dancing ability with my long limbs and unusual feet. To top it off, I felt very confident in dancing this important role.

"Night Island" premiered on January 20, 1955 in The Hague. I was more excited than nervous, but Rudi was a complete nervous wreck. If you ask me how I felt during that first performance, I could not tell you. I remember the start, and then it was over. I was relieved the performance went well and we received a standing ovation with many "bravos." People came backstage and could not stop talking about it. The positive reaction was such a welcome surprise, one that overwhelmed me. The next day Rudi read the raving reviews about his *"Night Island"* from bed because he got himself sick from all the tension and built-up nerves, a problem that continued his whole life. The reviews not only talked about Rudi's exceptional job as a choreographer, but also about how well we danced it. Rudi and I were interviewed for television and that was more nerve-racking than dancing the ballet

itself. On camera, I was unable to put into words how personal the ballet was for me, because they would have asked me why. Since I was hiding my true feelings, I had a difficult time discussing "*Night Island*" during the interview. Afterward Rudi confirmed what I was feeling and said I didn't make any sense. When I asked him what I said, since I could not recall it, he replied that he could not remember either. We both fell to the floor in laughter.

Rudi and I were as close as family to each other. As our dance careers continued to propel forward our parents seemed to slip into the background. Rudi's parents did not attend opening night to see their son's major accomplishment. Needless to say, he was very hurt. Their excuse was that The Hague was too far and unknown. The real reason was that they were, "People shy," Rudi explained. "They just don't know how to act if they are around strangers."

Although I had told my parents all about the ballet and how important it was to me, they did not attend either. Their lack of interest was a painful blow. They told me it was too difficult to take the one-hour train ride to The Hague. I think they didn't want to spend the money. Therefore, from this point on, I never told them what I was working on, and that was that. This was the same for the rest of my extended family. For the entire eleven years I danced in Holland, only one aunt, my Uncle Rein's wife Jo and daughter, Angemieke, came to see me perform. Uncle Rein was Mom's brother. None of my other aunts and uncles or my half-sisters, Leny and Henny, ever came to the theater to see me perform. They saw me dance on television, so I assume that was enough. The concept of going to a dance performance must have been too foreign to them. I would like to believe they were proud when they saw me on television, but I am not sure.

This was the beginning of a remarkable career for Rudi as a choreographer. He would go on to become artistic director of The National Ballet, and choreographed for major dance companies all over the world. It was also the beginning of a wonderful career for me as a dancer. I owed a lot of it to Rudi because he believed in my ability to portray what he envisioned for *Night Island*. My roles in his subsequent ballets displayed more of what I had in me. I grew as a dancer and became strong on stage. I attribute much of this to Rudi. I loved dancing his ballets, and the ballets of every other choreographer who entrusted me to perform their work. It was an honor, and gave me enormous pleasure. I didn't become world famous, but that is okay with me.

SIXTEEN

Paris

My life was not always serious and dance driven, I had a light-hearted side as well. I was a sixteen-year-old teenager, and Rudi who was older, acted like one. Speaking of all the influences Rudi had on me, this was not a good one. We often snuck into theaters to see dance and various performances. Since we were dodging paying admission to these performances, these trips to the theaters were always an adventure, From hiding in theatre attics, to muffling laughter mixed with fear when we were on the brink of getting caught, to the sheer freedom of being young and rambunctious together.

During this time, I was obsessed with Paris because many famous people in the ballet world resided and worked there. Marianna and Jaap went there to take classes with the famous ballet instructor Madame Egorova, a teacher who instructed Mevrouw when she was younger. Everyone who visited the so called City of Light talked endlessly about the special times they had there and how beautiful the city was. I saw Paris as a kind of Shangri-La. When I passed a parked tour bus from Paris on my bike, I would let my fingers slide along its side to get some Paris dirt on them. I thought this was as close to Paris as I would ever get. My luck soon changed when Rudi asked me to join him and his family for a week in Paris. I could not be happier!

We arrived by train and found a spacious room in a cheap hotel where we ate and slept. We visited all the museums and saw all the famous sights, including climbing to the top of the Eiffel Tower. By coincidence we met the brother of the famous dancer, Isadora Duncan. He was recited poems wearing Greek robes and sandals on the banks of the Seine River. I didn't understand a word he spook, but was still amazed because he was the brother of a famous modern dancer.

Of course, when you are in Paris you must buy French perfume. I asked Rudi to help me in my search since he spoke French well. I took French in school, but to go into a store and talk to a real French woman was a little terrifying. Rudi urged me to face my fears and encouraged me, "No, you can do it." Before I knew it, I was proudly walking out of that store with my bottle of Femme, au de toilette. I loved perfume ever since smelling it on Mevrouw. Femme smelled a little like hers, but not quite the same. I don't know why I never just asked her what perfume she wore.

Every evening we ate the same meal in our substantial hotel room. We felt very Parisian walking back after a wonderful day of site-seeing with a couple of French breads tucked under our arms. A camp stove provided the vehicle we needed to cook up onions, garlic, green peppers, tomatoes, and eggs. Cooking was a team effort combined with lots of laughter while reminiscing about the day's events. Evening walks in Paris was something I loved. There was so much going on; it felt like we had joined a party. Every person in this beautiful city seemed to be outside, either walking around or sitting on terraces having a marvelous time in a sea of lights. One evening we went to see the movie *Ivan the Terrible*, in a Moroccan theater. Standing in line in a half lit hallway, surrounded by French-speaking strangers in a Moroccan atmosphere, going to see a Russian movie with French subtitles… how exciting and worldly! I loved it all, including our daily evening meals. I loved it so much that I brought everything, minus the eggs, back to Holland to cook for my parents. I made it for them, but it just wasn't the same. The Paris magic had disappeared from it.

SEVENTEEN

On My Own

After the first year of the company's existence, the city of The Hague decided to subsidize *The Netherlands Ballet,* thus making the company relocate to that city. My parents thought I was still too young to live in The Hague by myself. A dancer friend named Ria Leeuwerik lived with a family in The Hague, and they didn't mind if I also came to stay with them. This was a short-lived living situation since I had to pay them just about all the money I made. Ria and I felt we could do better on our own so we found two rooms in the house of a woman who owned a textile store. That was it; I was on my own living in a tiny room overlooking a garden. It was furnished and we had access to the kitchen. With my small radio, bought on credit, I was feeling very independent and content at the age of sixteen. I was proud to stand on my own two feet.

All of the dancers who didn't have their families in The Hague were living in rental rooms. Post war hardships still lingered amongst the Dutch so renting out rooms in their houses was means to earn additional income and make ends meet. Typically, these rooms were the tiniest in the house and privacy was something of the past. All those components of renting allowed for many amusing stories amongst the dancers.

Personally, I did not care for my landlady. She wanted to know everything about my comings and goings and because I didn't want to tell her my personal business, she didn't like me either.

On the other hand, she loved Ria. The woman showered her with big chocolate bonbons every day, and made sure I knew about it. I had it with the woman and left, Ria stayed. My next rental was an attic room in the neighborhood of The Hague where all the streets are named after Indonesian Islands. Sometime later, when two additional rooms in the attic became available two more dancers moved in. One of them was Gaby, who was still one of my best friends. I was thrilled to have her so close to me and essentially housemates.

In the second year of The Netherlands Ballet, Toer van Schayk joined the company. Toer, then a young man of twenty, was tall, dark and handsome. Besides Rudi, Toer was the most gifted person I had ever met. Multi-talented was an understatement when it came to Toer; from a phenomenal dancer, to a painter, sculptor, choreographer and an incredible set designer. Eventually, Rudi and Toer became a couple. Though they didn't stay together, their friendship and working relationship went on for the rest of Rudi's life. I was very fond of Toer and developed a close friendship with him as well. The three of us spent much of our free time together and shared many memories. Sometimes after our dinner, we took walks in a big park in The Hague close to where I lived. One evening in that park we were lying in the grass talking, while gazing up at the stars. Rudy and Toer were lying on either side of me when a police officer approached shining a flashlight in our faces. The officer asked me if I was all right. He probably thought we were doing a threesome hokey-pokey in the grass. Good thing we weren't wrestling or else he would not have believed me. Wrestling, playing jokes or just being young together was what made our friendship easy and playful. Sometimes on our walks, we passed some homes where windows were too high to look into living rooms, I would climb on top of Rudi and Toer's shoulders and pass by as if I was a giant. The bewildered residents would receive a cool nod but a few blocks later, we would tumble to the sidewalk in fits of laughter. Even though I didn't think so at the time, those years were precious.

During these years, friends were quickly becoming family and my parents seemed more distant, not just in proximity but also in closeness. I realized that I longed for a closer relationship with my parents, most especially my mother. Seeing my girl colleagues with their parents gave light to my feelings and at times made me jealous of what they had.

Since Gaby and I were close friends, naturally her family became part of my life as well. Her mother Phyllis, who was divorced, was a fierce disciplinarian with her daughter and two sons. She also had a soft side I could relate to. Phyllis became my second mother. I could tell her everything, that is everything except my secret. I think I was closer to her than she was with her own daughter. Gaby and her mother were complete opposites. I admired Phyllis strength and trusted her advice, confident she would not steer me wrong. The older I got, the more we did things together, and would talk for hours. Phyllis remained my close friend and confidante for the remainder of her life. Years later, she developed breast cancer and ended her life with the help of her doctor. Euthanasia is allowed in Holland when all hope of survival is completely gone. We spoke on the phone to say our forever goodbyes. It was the saddest phone call I ever made. It was so difficult to hang up the phone knowing it would be a final time.

My feelings for my own parents at this time in my life remained shaky. I was a teenager, so this was not unusual. Most teens go against their parents as a way of finding themselves, but for me there was also the secret. My understanding about the NSB became even clearer over the years. It had made me more ashamed and angry with my parents.

I got along with Papa, but I could not stand Mom. Maybe this sounds too harsh, but don't forget all the hard times I endured as a little girl during the war and immediately after. All of those memories were mostly with my mother. Besides, I didn't trust her. Before I moved to The Hague and was still living at home, Mom went through my things. She did that with Papa as well, which irritated me. One afternoon I was sitting in the living room talking with a friend from school. My friend mentioned that her parents were so nosey. I said, "I know what you mean. Right now my mother is listening and looking at us through that hole in the door." With that, Mom opened the door laughing as if it was a joke. Conscious of her sneaky ways, I knew she was spying on us.

I have often wondered why my parents never asked me if the events before the war, during and post have affected me in any way. Their lack of compassion or interest in me and my feelings I now see as weak and cowardly. Maybe that is the reason why they joined the N.S.B. in the first place. Now that I was a teenager, I thought it was the right time to find out why we had joined this group, and on one of my weekend visits I discussed it with my mother. I tried to express how upsetting all this had been for me. I told her about the nightmares, and how I can still see her disappearing in that car, which had been a terrible real life nightmare. One would think a mother would express sympathy for her child during a discussion like ours, but that did not happen.

She tossed it away with, "Well, it's something I'd like to forget."

"It is not something I can forget so easily," I said. "That horrible stinking school prison they put me in was hell! If I had not tried to get out of that place myself, Aunt Jo would not have come to get me. Maybe I would still be there, or maybe dead."

"What do you mean?" she asked.

"Never mind, I would rather not explain it. It's all because of you!"

She was quiet and didn't respond with any sympathy. Then, I asked the question that had been on my mind for so long now. "Why did we join those horrible people in the first place?"

Shock quickly replaced my curiosity when my mother simply replied, "We did it for you."

From that moment forward, those words were branded in my

memory. I felt guilty enough already and now I was the reason for it all. I never forgave my parents for not apologizing. I didn't bother discussing this topic with my mother ever again because I realized I would never get the truth from her anyway.

Dance was my savior, a kind of fever within me. I focused on that and buried my past baggage deep within. My parents had indulged my desire to dance, so for that I am grateful. They were there when I needed a home on my free weekends. I just never got the emotional support I expected from my parents, especially from my Mom.

I was eighteen when my Mom developed cancer and needed a hysterectomy. After the operation, she had complications and had to remain in the hospital for four weeks. Papa had never taken care of himself. The extent of his cooking was brewing a pot of tea. I decided to ride the train to Amsterdam on days I didn't have a performance and take care of Papa. The shopping, cooking and cleaning all became my duties. I found the laundry to be the most tiresome since we did not own a washing machine. Lugging the soiled clothes numerous blocks to the laundromat was not enjoyable.

Papa appreciated my hard work and would treat me to pastries and sometimes a movie after our hospital visits on weekends. Papa allotted me the same weekly money he gave Mom to take care of the household. I had thought I was doing as good of a job as my mother while she recovered in the hospital. Of course Mom told me otherwise. With a huge grin on her face, she informed me that Papa said she did everything much better. Why would she say this? I was doing my best to take care of things while working around my own schedule all the while commuting between The Hague and Amsterdam. Comments like this were what pushed me further away from my mother.

That same year my parents decided to go to Knokke, Belgium for Christmas. I understood their need to get away after Mom's ordeal but did it have to be at Christmas? They didn't ask me if

I wanted to go with them, but they did ask me if I would mind if they went. With my personality, I answered those questions only with what they wanted to hear. In response, they suggested I spend the holidays with my friends. I was too ashamed to ask my friends who were all celebrating Christmas with their families, so instead I stayed in my attic room and cooked myself a nice dinner. I decided to go to the Christmas mass held in a nearby church. I am not religious; it was more the desire to be surrounded by people. I liked the music but did not care very much for anything else during the mass. It was too commercial with that little collection basket poking parishioners faces for this and then for that. Afterwards, I felt so lonely walking back home in the cold dark night. Noticing I was by myself, someone asked me if I needed a ride when I left the church. I declined but would have liked to say yes if tears were not already streaming down my face.

EIGHTEEN

Rising Through The Ranks

The year after the debut of *Night Island*, Rudi was commissioned to produce a new ballet. We were dance partners now, and Rudi lined us up to dance this ballet together. The ballet was about two people whose cold mundane lives are changed with the appearance of the moon. The moon replaces their reality with tenderness and love until the moon disappeared and brings back all that they so desperately want to leave behind. My role was romantic and lyrical, the complete opposite of what I was in *Night Island*. I now realized how much I liked to become the part I danced, making it understandable to the audience.

The ballet, *Tide and Tideless*, was another success. The reviews were very favorable, not only because of the choreography and the dancing, but also because of Toer's set and costume designs. Rudi and Toer were lucky in the fact that they were able to maintain a close friendship and an equally strong working relationship. From this ballet on Toer designed the sets and costumes for all of Rudi's future ballets.

The Dutch Royal Family was very fond of dance and would occasionally be in the audience of our performances. On those occasions, there would be a reception with the Queen following the performance to meet Mevrouw, Jaap and Marianna. After all, they were the stars of the company. Just standing in the same room with royalty was momentous, but what I savored most was the delicious morsels to eat. Another opportunity was presented to our company in which we performed for Queen Juliana's twenty-fifth wedding anniversary. Much like the cherry on top of a delicious sundae, we were invited to join the party afterwards. The celebration was the cornucopia of the horn-of-plenty. As a matter of fact, there was an actual horn-of-plenty, spilling over with bright red strawberries dipped in milk chocolate. I had never seen such luxury! With an unending flow of sumptuous food and drink, and everyone dressed to the nines.

Rudi and I in *Tide and Tideless*.

From time to time, there were post-performance cocktail parties and receptions given by so-called important people. So my need for cocktail dresses became essential. Luckily, I was friends with our company's costumier Ger Frenzen. He enjoyed designing clothes, so if I paid for the material, he made my dresses. They were fancy all right. I even had a satin dress in a shocking pink! I was hard to miss. The best parties, however, were always with the dancers, either in the studio or in each other's houses. We never drank alcohol, the thought never even entered my mind. I did have a bottle of wine in my attic room. I had bought it for my parents in Germany while on a performance tour. I was alone one evening and thought, I wonder what it feels like to be drunk. I decided to find out. I opened the bottle, and took a few sips. When I started to feel a little funny and different I thought, so this is the effect alcohol has on you, whoopee. That was the end of my drinking for quite a while.

Every year each dancer met with the business director of the company to sign a new contract. When it came to self-worth, I was not outspoken enough to negotiate my salary. My thinking was that whatever this man felt I was worth was fine with me. I am sure he liked that. They got a lot of use out of me for little money. I did not realize until my last year with the company, dancers who demanded the most were paid the largest amounts.

The company was larger now. There were about forty-five dancers and some could be flat out horrid when they did not receive the roles they coveted. Competition between dancers was nasty and fierce at times, especially when it was over a lead role. Years later, I spoke about the competitiveness with fellow dancer Charles (Chuck) Csarny. I said to him that I was never jealous of any one that was chosen by the choreographer to dance his or her ballets. His answer was, "You didn't have to, because everything was just given to you." I had not thought about that, but he was right. Only one time I saw jealousy up close. The dancer, Job Sanders, came from New York to do guest performances and choreograph a ballet called *Street Corner Royalty*. It is about a bunch of hoodlums who, under the influence of drugs, dream about an ideal woman. Job chose me and another dancer to learn the part of the woman. Not happy that Job gave me most of his attention, my competition made it clear to me that she looked sexier than I did and had more experience with men. Initially by her boldness and accusations on my character hurt me. No one had ever put me down like that. In the end, I was chosen for the role and was doubly proud because I did not allow competitive bullying ruin my spirit and affect my dancing.

During my years with the company, we danced all the classics. Famous people in the ballet world, including David Lichine, taught those ballets to us. Mevrouw told us that Mr. Lichine had been quite the ladies' man in his younger years while dancing with the Diaghilev Ballet Company. We got a glimpse of his flirtatious nature while working on his ballet. Lichine always had a twinkle in his eyes as if he had just heard or told a little joke. I assumed this to be true because Mevrouw, who always sat beside him, laughed and behaved like a young girl when he whispered in her ear. Maybe they were flirting, who knows. He was kind of a spoiled man. He wanted a big steak for lunch every day, and the dancers had to cook it. We only ate steak on special occasions, so when Mr. Lichine did not finish his delectable piece of meat, we were irritated. When it was my turn to cook, I was not happy about it. I threw the steak to Rudi and said, "You do it." With a laugh he threw it back to me, and then the trouble started. As the distance between steak tossing increased so did the amount of dancers who joined in for the fun. Naturally, the steak fell on the floor a couple of times. Now I cooked Mr. Lichine's lunch with pleasure, and we all enjoyed watching him savor each bite.

Mevrouw also invited Leonide Massine to work with us. He was also a famous dancer and choreographer with the Diaghilev Ballet and one of the leading actors in the movie *The Red Shoes.* The movie I had seen years ago and had loved. Massine was not very tall, but had a powerful presence and beautiful dark brown eyes. He picked me out in class to do a leading part in his ballet *Fifth Symphony.* I was very honored to be selected by such a famous person. I could tell he liked me as a dancer. Later, when he came back to set *Petroesjka*, he choose me again to dance the devil. We even wore the original costumes of *Petroesjka* from the Diaghilev Ballet Company. The costumes had been stored in Paris during the war years, and now were shipped to us. Unpacking them from big leather travel trunks, we were like kids in a candy store. The idea that they once belonged to this famous ballet company and now we would be wearing them was so thrilling! The absolutely lovely costumes were constructed in fabrics from silks, to plush velvets and even fur.

Leonide Massine with the costumes of
Petroesjka from the Diaghilev Ballet Company.

Rudi was continuing to be successful with his ballets and I loved the roles I danced in them. It was dancing his ballet, *Those At Table,* when I had the revelation that I would have loved to be an actress if I was not already a dancer.

Gaby and I in Paris.

My summer vacations were not spent on the beach with Aunt Gre. Although she was one of my favorite aunts, so easy going and always fun to be around, I had other interests now. These summers I spent with my friends. Gaby's brother was working in a restaurant in Paris, and we decided to go see him. We got a cheap hotel room that turned out to have cockroaches. Every time we turned the light on those bugs were all over the place. Gaby, who knew a little more French than me, tried to explain our situation to the manager. Gaby displayed fingers sprouting from either side of her head in attempt to illustrate to the man insect antennas, just as Mevrouw made us do when we were the Ants. We broke out into hysterics at the Ants memory. The owner pretended not to understand. After that, we slept with all the lights on.

Gaby and I in dressing room before a performance.

We did our sightseeing by walking everywhere. It was a different time, and the strangest thing was that men pinched our behinds. For fun, we kept count. Gaby was the winner of most pinches. This was understandable because Gaby was, in Rudi's words, a Hitte Petitje—blonde and on the sexy side. We asked Gaby's brother why men were doing that in Paris since it didn't happen in Holland. He told us he didn't have that trouble so he couldn't say. Having Gaby's brother in Paris was reassuring and also helpful since he showed us sites and exposed us to the French culture. Thanks to him, we went to see the *Folies Bergère*, a famous Paris variety show. Our sides ached from laughter. I never thought watching bare-breasted singing women on big flower-covered swings would be so entertaining. I had the feeling that my Aunt Cor thought I was doing something similar like that for a living.

NINETEEN

Trouble In The Company

The Netherlands Ballet Company had quickly become too large and complicated for one person to handle. Evidence of that could be seen each day after the morning class. Mevrouw refused to put up a rehearsal schedule for the day. Dancers lolled about the studio waiting to hear from Mevrouw whether or not they would be rehearsing. Many times you did nothing but wait. It was especially hard to abruptly begin rehearsing a ballet on toe after sitting in the cantina drinking tea and chatting for hours... Out of pure frustration and boredom, Rudi and I would resort to our silly antics. For instance, we would have someone announce to Mevrouw that a Russian couple was there to see her. Rudi and I would then strut in dressed like Russian babushkas or whatever we could think of, Mevrouw would tolerate our stunts and found them humorous but only to a point. When she had enough she would holler, "Rudi and Hannie, damn it." From that point on "damn it" became our last name.

One time, on a beautiful day, Rudi Toer and I called in sick and headed to the beach for the day. When we returned the following day pink and sun kissed, Mevrouw was speechless but certainly knew. Our misbehaving stemmed from our unhappiness of how things were run in the company. In a way, Mevrouw was behaving the way I had when I refused to wear a hairnet so long ago, like a stubborn child. Rudi and I were not the only ones, a very large group of dancers were growing increasingly frustrated with the woman we once adored. Mevrouw wanted complete control; to teach classes, run rehearsals and be the artistic and business director. We had a business director by the name of Carel Birnie who wanted to arrange things better for the dancers. She didn't want to listen and in the end fired him. This all happened on the end of the season on tour in Germany. There we, the dancers, gave Mevrouw a list of changes we deemed important. One of those things was getting Mr. Birnie back.

Without delving too deep into the politics of our dance company, things ended hellish at the start of our vacation. We received some shocking news upon our return from August break. Mevrouw sat us down and informed us that she had hired a new business director and had found a teacher in New York who was highly recommended. He would handle her tasks of teaching and rehearsing. Milly Gramberg, a dancer from the Opera ballet who had just joined us, asked the question that hung from our lips, "Are you not going to be here to work with us?" Mevrouw's short reply was that she wanted to visit many places and take time to see interesting things. With that, she walked to the door, her words hovering over us like heavy storm clouds leaving us speechless. The room was silent.

A couple of days later we were introduced to Benjamin Harkarvy, our new ballet master. He was not what you would expect a dance teacher to look like. Harkarvy was young, with a round body and a bold round head like a bowling ball, but I loved his lessons. Mevrouw stayed true to her word and left for Paris where she gave the board of directors her resignation. It was not what she wanted of course but she wanted to give the board and us a good scare. The board asked her to rethink her decision and take six months off for a so-called "rest"

Filled with excitement and anticipation, we thought things would run more smoothly because of the changes. Unfortunately, that was wishful thinking. Mevrouw's micromanagement reigned even in her absence. She informed both Benjamin Harkarvy and the new business director man Jan Huckriede how to run the company through a letter. Her letter began with, "These are my rules I want you to follow." Benjamin Harkarvy ignored her wishes and with the help of dancer Aart Verstegen things got much better. They were able to make the company run smoothly. However, Mevrouw still had eyes and ears within the studio and certainly was not pleased that her demands were ignored. When her time in Paris came to an end, she returned to the studio and things resumed to the way they were before she left. Mevrouw's way was the law, the dancers and everyone else had to obey, including Benjamin Harkarvy.

TWENTY

Starting Anew

There was a buzz around the studio that the veteran dancer, Aart Verstegen, our former business manager Carel Birnie, and Benjamin Harkarvy had the idea of starting a new company. Soon after Harkarvy asked if I wanted to become a part of this new Netherlands Dance Theater. Once I heard who else was joining the new company, I whole-heartedly said, "Yes!" Even though the future of the company was unpredictable, I had faith that Carel Birnie would make it successful and I already knew what a talented teacher Ben was. The rest was up to us dancers. We were a talented group and I knew it was only a matter of time before we had the audience behind us.

At the end of the year, I wrote my letter informing the board that I would not be returning next season. When Mevrouw heard who was leaving, she treated us like air and never said another word to me.

Looking back, my nineteen-year-old- self did not see this as a major step. I was young and willing to take chances. However, this time in my life was one of major change. It was an end of an era; my Mevrouw days were over. My thought was, what happens, happens; if we freeze to death, we freeze to death.

Rehearsals for the new company commenced before our contracts with *The Netherlands Ballet* had expired. Thus, those rehearsals were held in secret. Without a studio of our own, the new company rented space in a couple of dance schools in The Hague.

Every one received the same salary of 250 guilders a month, which was less than half the amount I made prior. It was no problem for me. I was accustomed to living on just about nothing anyway. By month's end, I do recall counting pennies, which was tough. Biking home after rehearsals, being accosted by the delicious aromas of dinners from the passing houses I passed was torture for my empty stomach. I longed for an invite to any one of their tables. However, the exciting work with the new company erased the hardships that came with a lesser salary.

On September 5, 1959 a couple of days before our Dutch official opening, we had a performance in the Kurhaus Theatre of Oostende, Belgium. *Giovinezza*, created by Rudi was our opening ballet. It is an Italian renaissance ballet for eight dancers. When the plush red curtain rose we were all standing or sitting frozen in a pose. The Vivaldi music starts and one by one we exits the stage until three dancers are left. I was first and made a big Port de bras get up from my kneeling position and walk off. What I realized later was that I was the first one who started the dancing in the company. That was the start of everything. Now it has a first and second company and has a worldwide reputation. The performance in Belgium was a tremendous success. Afterwards Hanny Bouman, our ballet mistress, and I drove back to Holland in her little open sports car. The wind blowing in our hair, and giggling the whole way home while reminiscing about our performance.

All of us were the so-called Rebel Dancers of this new company. Six of the dancers I grew up with were, Mable, Jaap, Marianna, Willy, Aart and Rudi. Ten dancers I had danced with at The Netherlands Ballet also became part of the new company. A little while later Hans van Manen joined and brought the wonderful French dancer Gerard le Maitre with him. Toer didn't join because he was concentrating on his sculpting and painting, but he was still making set and costume designs for Rudi's ballets. All of us were very much like a family. We relied on each other to not only make this work, but to make it successful.

Septet: Charles Czarny, Gerard
Lemaitre and myself in Milan.

A few days after our Oostende performance the big day came
for opening night in Utrecht, The Netherlands. We had worked
hard and were ready for our Dutch judgment day. The public was
very much aware of why we started this new group. Newspapers
had been teeming with articles for about a year. Our dream came
true. We were an absolute sensation. As Martinette Janmaat, one
of our dancers, said years later with tongue in cheek, "It was the
beginning of our fame." Things were not a bed of roses since
we had numerous setbacks, but we always danced with a feverish
conviction. Bernie had over one hundred and fifty performances

booked for our first season. We worked timeless from early morning to late at night for months. Ben Harkarvy made new ballets one of which was called *Septet*. It was a ballet I loved to dance and one of his best ballets in my opinion.

When Ben Harkarvy was asked in an interview forty years later what convinced him to stay in Holland, he replied, "In the rebellious dancers of the Dutch Ballet, I have discovered a great sense of enthusiasm and a great sense of drama in the dance." The feeling the dancers had for him, he noted, was mutual. I felt very honored when he followed with,

When I saw Rudi van Dantzig's *Those At Table*, I knew for sure that I had to stay in the Netherlands. It's crazy how a subtle gesture on the stage can change your life dramatically. In my case, it was the gesture that Johanna van Leeuwen did in her role of the sister of a repudiated gay boy. It was a tense moment in the ballet when the parents disowned their son (by letting him drop on stage) because of his homosexuality. At that moment she pushed her friend away from her. With that gesture Johanna showed how much she loved her brother, even though she needed to comply with her parents and returned to their table on the platform. That immeasurable honesty she expressed with this simple movement moves me as much in my memory now as it did then. Nearly forty years later, I still see Johanna standing there in that light dress.

I know exactly the movement Ben spoke about. After reading my esteemed teacher's kind words all those years later, I had the acclamation I had strived for while dancing that ballet. It confirms that I was successful in making the audience understand what the choreography wanted to reveal with a small movement Rudi and I came up with. Just like in *Night Island*, we were very much in tune with each other.

Rudi, Jaap, Toer and I in *Those at Table*.

Annemarie Verhoeven, me, Jaap and
Aart Verstegen in *Those at Table*

TWENTY-ONE

Daily life

My attic apartment was still home to me, while the rest of the house was rented to normal people. ("Normal" is how we referred to non-dancers.)Dancers occupied all three attic rooms. Gaby was still there and the third room was occupied by Peter Paul Zwartjes, who like Gaby, was born in Indonesia. Gaby and Peter Paul had endless ghost stories to tell from that country. Nights when I was alone in the attic, I would lie awake haunted by their stories, imagining what could be on the other side of my door.

Gaby was dating the painter Jan Cremer. He was an abstract modern painter who had a big following in the art world. He often hosted parties at his house. Sometimes Gaby would drag me with her in hopes of me meeting someone. Little did she know I was petrified of letting anyone get close to me because of my secret. Gaby's matchmaking days did not last too long since within a year she had left dancing, ending her relationship with Cremer and moved to London.

A non-dancer girl named Liesbet came to live in Gaby's room. We became fast friends and I got to know her family as well. Her mother sent all the reviews about me that she could find. I was never interested in collecting them, but I did save the ones she sent, and I am happy I did. Liesbet had a brother who I really liked. We went out a couple of times, which was a mistake of me to do in the first place. I purposely sabotaged our relationship by making him feel that I was uninterested. I was heartbroken about it, but felt I had no other choice. It was better to end things sooner than later when I would have to divulge my shameful background. I was very mixed up, depressed, couldn't dance and had no appetite. Nothing kept my interest; it was one of my darkest times. My colleague and good friend Millie Gramberg's Mom took care of me for a while. Nobody knew what was wrong with me, but everyone was concerned, including Karel Birnie. He made an appointment for me to see a psychiatrist. I never went to the appointment because I was not prepared to tell anyone, including a doctor, about my secret. Eventually I worked myself out of this painful situation and saw it as a lesson to let it never happen again.

Internally, my secret had damaged me in the sense that I had little self-worth when it came to a love live. However, it did not damage my esteem when it came to my work and dancing. I didn't bend my knees anymore. Now I used my height to stand out and demanded attention from the audience. Sounds a bit self-centered but I felt it was my job as a professional dancer. Success on stage was not only for me to achieve, it was also for the choreographers who made the ballets and entrusted me to show the audience what they had envisioned. I was often used for mature roles when I was not even twenty, which I found quite humorous. When I questioned Ben Harkarvy as to why, he replied with, "Yes of course, because you are ageless on stage."

Throughout my dancing career, there were numerous ballets with distinct stories, more so than now. I am not referring about the classics, which universally use the arm and hand movements to convey emotions and their tales. I am talking about real modern plays where dancers expressed strong emotional subjects to the audience via dance. We were so fortunate to be able to work with the two incredibly talented young choreographers, Rudi van Dantzig and Hans van Manen, who brought stories to life on stage without a word. Lucky for me, I had the pleasure of dancing in five of Rudi's ballets. My first working relationship with

Hans was not until the opening of *Netherlands Dance Theater* in his ballet, *Party Judgment*. It is a story about a woman who is judged and persecuted by a mob of people. Rudi didn't sit still either; he choreographed *Vista*, a ballet about a woman who looks back on her live. I danced the role of this woman and four other dancers portrayed the different important times in my life. It was danced on Schumann's, Frauenliebe und Leben, the music that tells the story in German. I also had to recite a poem on the stage at the beginning of the ballet. I don't think that was ever done in a ballet before. We were a modern company with new ideas and the public liked that. We were well received all over the country, and it looked like the company had a future.

Even though I was thoroughly engaged in my dance life, I still made time to visit my parents. Hitchhiking was my method of returning home. Fortunately, I had the company of friends, my fellow dancers who were visiting family as well. Thus making these experiences more of an adventure. At that time there was not as much traffic in Holland as there is now so the wait for our future ride was often long and cold. We took drastic measures to keep warm, wearing articles of dance clothing in odd places, running on empty roundabouts late at night, or dancing and singing at the top of our lungs on a lonely highway. One time when a passerby finally stopped for us, Rudi quickly ran up to the side of the car with a leg warmer on his head. The frightened man took off as fast as he could. Hitchhikers were very common in Holland at the time so we did not worry about trouble with the authorities. Those fortunate enough to own a car usually would stop and pick up travelers like us, which made for fun memories.

Sunday visits with my parents were relaxing and enjoyable. Mom would do my dance laundry and I would relish in a meal that I did not have to prepare myself. Sometimes I was so exhausted, I would sleep most of the day only rousing for meals. Those Sundays I appreciated and cherished the most with my parents. After a restful visit, Rudi and I would hitchhike back Monday morning with clean clothes and a care package that would last me a couple of days. Sometimes while waiting for a ride, Mevrouw passed us in her little car on her way to The Hague. Of course she never stopped. Seeing her made me sad. She was Mevrouw after all, a woman you cannot let go of that easy. When we performed in The Hague, I always hoped she was there to see me dance, but I am sure that was only wishful thinking on my part.

TWENTY-TWO

Ducks Anyone?

Netherlands Dance Theater found an empty church in Den Haag that was suitable as a make shift studio. It was much too spacious so Aart Verstegen made a wall from old décor parts to make it work for us. That winter in our so-called studio it was bitterly cold. There was a stove, but since the place was so vast, it was not effective. Harry our pianist would strum the keys donned in his heaviest winter clothes, and wore woolen gloves with cut of fingertips to be able to feel the keys. At first glance the floor looked worn, but much to a dancer's delight, it had spring in it. Regardless of all its setbacks, I have the fondest memories dancing at that church.

Our church studio was enjoyable but short-lived, and by spring of 1960 we obtained a beautiful building called De Boterwaag in The Hague as our official studio. It was originally a weigh house for butter in the 17th Century. Well, we fell with our nose in the butter. (This Dutch expression means something good is happening to you). With ample space, we allotted the first floor to house the studio, dressing rooms, small kitchen and administration office. The basement was for sets and costumes. The dance floor was perfect but most important it had central heating.

Spring abounded everywhere. Flowers flourished, the breeze became warmer and gentler, and baby ducks were for sale at the market place. Rudi and I melted when we saw the fuzzy ducklings and decided to purchase two each. As novice parents we pondered what to feed them. We instinctively devised a diet of brown bread, leafy greens, and a sprinkle of cod-liver oil over everything. Unbelievably, the ducklings thrived with the exception of one of Rudi's who sadly died. I took on the remaining duckling as my own in fear that it would be too lonely. Now I was the proud owner of three ducklings who would cuddle at my feet or in the basket with a light over them for warmth. Soon they grew to the point that they were too much for me to handle by myself and too messy. Rudi and I had the marvelous idea to move them into the attic of De Boterwaag. Our feathered friends received light from a window and we made a fence for them, so they would have enough room to roam. The ducklings were also starting to change their voices, their peeps were becoming loud quacks and it cracked us up.

It must have been the Spring of Ducks for me and Rudi, since they seemed to be everywhere these days. One afternoon we were performing on an open-air stage perched on the edge of a small lake. The public sat across the lake and munched on tea and crumpets while enjoying the performance. To us, it seemed like the audience was too far away to understand, let alone see us. On top of that, one of the ballets on the program was Rudi's *Night Island*. What a choice for a tea drinking audience. While we were dancing it, we suddenly heard a peep turning into a quack, just like our ducklings! We just started the ballet and saw a flock of ducks waddling towards the stage. Soon they were part of our performance peeping and quacking amongst Rudi and myself. We could not contain our laughter and didn't even think about hiding it from the audience, who seemed too far off to even know what was happening. Afterwards, Harkarvy told us that he had heard us loud and clear and wasn't very happy about it. It was "Rudi and Hannie Damn it," all over again.

As far as our ducks were concerned, they were plump, messy and foul smelling. To make matters worse, bugs had taken up residence in the attic as well. Carel Birnie caught wind of it, literally, and told us to get rid of them. We brought the ducks to a children's park where they were cared for. The care takers put them in a cage at first to let them get acclimated with their new surroundings before allowing them to be with other resident ducks. We could not believe it when they were given only a little cup with seeds in their cage. We questioned if they knew what they were doing, but I think it must have been the other way around. I said we would visit them, but never did. Cleaning the disgusting attic cured us of our duck desire. In our hearts we knew we had saved them and that was all that mattered to us. To this day, whenever I see ducks a smile spreads over my face, I think of my good friend Rudi and of course our feathered friends and chuckle to myself.

Two of our ducks on newspaper with an article about Dance Theater. The photo behind the right duck is me in *Septet*.

TWENTY-THREE

———— ❦ ————

One Foot Forward

The majority of our time was spent working. We danced all over Holland on the grandest of stages in cities and quaint theaters in tiny villages. The variety of stage floors we encountered over the years were challenging at times. Some sloped while others had holes or splinters to deal with. Some stages were so minuscule that when your partner lifted you, the audience saw you headless. We endured these nuances to earn money of course and to get ourselves known throughout the country. I trusted Carel Birnie. He was a man who knew all the ins and outs of the law. At one point when things were really looking bleak money wise, he made us stand in the unemployment line while we were still working. How he did things and got away with them baffled me, he certainly was a shrewd businessman. Our hard work and dedication got us so far with success, but without Carel I don't think the company would be where it is now.

New Ballets were always in the works since they helped build our repertoire and established our company. One of our more successful ballets was a jazz ballet called, *"Ready Set Go,"* by Hans van Manen, with music by Duke Ellington. It was so popular people bellowed for an encore. We would meet their demands repeating the finale of the ballet. Much to our delight, this happened quite often. *"Ready Set Go,"* not only enthralled the spectators but it was also a blast for us to dance. Hans put a lot of clever, fun things into it. The ballet had four parts. The opening was with all of us, than there were two pas de deus, one of which I danced with Jaap. Then the finale was with all of us again and by then all hell broke loose with excitement from the audience. The ballet reminds me of a little fun Hans and I had with playing tag. Wherever we were, in class or in a rehearsal, where we couldn't avoid each other we would tag and say, "You're it." In "*Ready Set Go*", Hans begins the ballet by sitting low on one knee in total darkness in the middle of the stage. The rest of us are all ready to go, the music starts and just before the curtain goes up, I sneak behind him, tap him on the shoulder and proclaim, "You're it." That one could not be beat, and ended our tag.

Ready Set Go, with most of the members
of the Netherlands Dance Theater.

Our company began to gain recognition from the audience but not always from the dance critics writing for the Dutch newspapers. Some were for Mevrouw and wanted to do us harm with their critique. Lucky for us, any negativity did not affect filling the audience for performances. To top it off, Hans had won a prize for his ballet, *"Party Judgement,"* and one of the Dutch TV stations was interested in airing it. Television obviously allowed us to reach a much larger audience, but first we had to do a six-week tour in Israel.

TWENTY-FOUR

Israel

We departed for Israel in October of our second season. Since we had to be economical, the trip itself was lengthy and tiresome. First, we took the train from The Hague to Marseille, a trip that took a day. There we had to wait to get on a freighter, filled with immigrants going to their promised land. Carel was able to secure us a reduced fare since we were the entertainment for the trip. We were stuck on this boat for six days and bored stiff most of the day. However, I did enjoy doing a ballet barre on the ship's railing every morning. Standing with the warm sun on our faces, the salt air filling our lungs and the beautiful azure water as our endless scenery was pretty magical and extraordinary. Instead of just counting out for our exercises, Ben always made a melody out of it when we didn't have our pianist. On that boat giving us a barre, he sounded more jubilant than ever. Performances on the moving boat were a whole new experience and needless to say, a challenge. Dancing and trying to balance on toe shoes on a moving boat was not easy, especially with a new partner. It felt like something else was controlling my body and that something was the boat. Rudi didn't come to Israel at first because he said that he was sick when we left. I know it was because he had issues with Ben, and that made him unhappy in the company. I was upset with him because I had to dance, *"Night Island"* in his absence with Aart.

We were accustomed to our busy work schedule but there was nothing to do on the boat but lie in the sun and read. To most, this would be a welcome reprieve but to us the lack of structure and work was beginning to get to us. Mealtimes became the highlight of the day. When the food bell clanked, we all jumped up. It was funny walking together as a group on the deck of the crazy rocking boat. We swayed back and forth like a bunch of Charley Chaplins, as if performing a dance that was never choreographed or rehearsed, but somehow we all knew it.

When we finally arrived in Israel, our home base was Haifa. We stayed in a hotel at first but there were so many large bugs crawling around, we couldn't stand it. Throughout the tour, I spent most of my time with Milly, Hans and Gerard and very little with Rudi who had joined us in Israel a couple of weeks later. I agreed with Rudi with some of the issues he had with Ben, but I did not want to sacrifice *Netherlands Dance Theater* because of it. One issue was of course that both Ben and Marianna secretly received a salary of 1000 guilders a month instead of 250 like everyone else. The rest of the issues were personal between Rudi and Ben and I thought that Rudi was making it a bigger deal then necessary . The whole situation rubbed off on me and made me disconcerted with Rudi and Ben. In turn, Rudi was upset with me since I did not spend time with him.

We danced in open-air theaters quite often and the lights attracted the biggest insects you ever wanted to see. Needless to say we avoided stepping on them at all cost since the sheer thought of the crunch under our feet gave us the shivers, so we danced around them. I started to think that all Israeli men were very horny because in those open-air theaters we spied them peering through every crack in the walls of our dressing rooms. They were even brazen enough to crawl under the floor planks.

From Haifa, we bussed everywhere, dancing in the big cities of Tel Aviv and Jerusalem, but also in smaller places like Kibbutz. The people of the smaller cities were always very hospitable, typically hosting a post-performance party, or inviting us to share a meal. On one occasion while we visited *The Inbalim Dance Company*, I was sitting on the floor and remember hearing a loud thud next to me. Cautiously I looked over to investigate and saw a scorpion sticking out on either side of a man's shoe. Luckily, he saw the scorpion first; otherwise, I would have been stung!

On the days we did not have a performance, we would retreat to the beach after rehearsals. Our beach time was more of exploration than relaxation. This beach was nothing like those in The Netherlands. It was completely covered with hundreds of holes filled with crabs of all sizes. They would surface when we laid still and occasionally one popped up from under our blankets. Tomato skins were abundant on the beach as well as floating in the water. All the sewers of Haifa emptied directly into the Mediterranean Sea at that time. While this fact was disgusting and far from comforting, we swam there anyway. I had seen a lot worse than tomato skins in the water during my life. The only thing I was surprised about was that the people in Israel ate so many tomatoes. Rudi asked what I was doing when he saw me rolling myself onto the beach. I told him, "I am pretending to be a turd that is washing ashore." Over our lifetime, I have heard him tell that story to many different people numerous times, each time more humorous than the last.

During our six week stay in Israel we had a handful of days off, one of which we used to visit the Dead Sea. It has become a tourist destination with numerous hotels and resorts, but at that time in 1960, it was as bare and colorless as the moon. We were the only ones around except for two women completely covered in dark grey mud. It was quite far and very difficult to walk to the water through this thick dark mud. Sometimes your step stayed close to the top of the mud but your next made you sink to your knee in that muddy earth. When we finally managed to get in the water, it was indeed an experience. I was happy that nothing could live in this water because feeling the mud mushing through your toes and the water as murky as the night was not very inviting. Milly and I were taught to swim like frogs but with each bend of our knees, our behinds jutted high out of the extremely salty water. Buoyancy was on our side and realized there was no need to swim. We were weightless as if we were really on the moon. Milly and I were fully enjoying our Dead Sea experience until we noticed poor Hans panicking to get out of the water. With each step, he struggled and sunk deeper into the mud all the while hissing through his teeth and grasping his neck in sheer agony. Unfortunately, he had shaved that morning and that very salty water was the cause of his misery. The whole scene had Milly and I in hysterics, it was a good thing we could not drown in that water. When we all got out, we dried quickly from the intense heat. Every piece of body hair had a salt cluster attached to it, which was extremely uncomfortable.

Our driver who had taken us to the sea kindly informed us about a little spring where we could wash away the salt. We couldn't wait! The spring consisted of a small wooden tub about five feet by five feet wide with a steady little stream of mineral water flowing from a rocky wall. The water transformed this wall into a mirage of sorts, which displayed all the colors of the rainbow. It was such simple beauty in this barren moonscape. We lowered ourselves into the tub and joined a woman who was already enjoying the refreshing water. There we sat, on top of one another, in a hole in the middle of nowhere. Steeling glances from one to another, we sat in silence with the trickle of the little stream coming out of the rocks as our background noise. A nervous giggle slowly erupted amongst us and soon became unbearable to contain. The poor woman thought we were laughing at her and abruptly exited the tub giving us a dirty look in her wake. Later Milly confessed that she laughed so hard she peed in the tub. We burst into another bout of hysterics with this news. Still to this day, I look back at Israel and smile at all of the memories. For the company, the Israel tour was a success. Our audiences thoroughly enjoyed the modern ballets, in particular, "*Night Island.*" Personally, I received a substantial amount of recognition and was cited as one of the best dancers in the company. This is not coming from me, but from an interview Carel Birnie gave in Holland when we got back.

TWENTY-FIVE

━━━━━ ⧢οⵖ ━━━━━

Ups And Downs

The morale and situation within the company was pretty lousy upon our return from tour. Rudi's relationship with Ben Harkavy hit a new low. For Rudi it was enough to leave the company and return to *The Netherlands Ballet*. Mevrouw took him back with open arms. I was also perturbed by the fact that Ben and Marianna had received more money than the rest of us, but to go back to Mevrouw was the last thing I wanted to do. Besides, who knows if she had wanted me back anyway.

Netherlands Dance Theater had come to a point that made Ben think we were doomed. I was livid because without any discussion with the company, Ben arranged for us to become members of a new company that was the product of merging *The Ballet of the Low Country,* and *The Opera Ballet*; the two remaining companies besides *The Netherlands Ballet* in Holland. When we heard that Jaap and Willy had already signed up, we all filled out an application for this new company that would be located in Amsterdam. I could not believe Ben was giving up so easily. Although I was accepted into the new company for the next season, I could not see myself there. I relied very much on Carel to come up with a solution that would save us. Marianna did not agree with this merge and left to work in Paris. She was a big loss for the company. Our advertisements now read "Farewell Performances," something none of us liked. Our audiences were saddened as well. We had acquired a rather large following who enjoyed our work immensely, which was apparent by the standing ovations we received after each performance.

There was turmoil within the government about what to do with these two big ballet companies, one in The Hague and the new one forming in Amsterdam. In the end, supporting two big companies was too costly so the decision was to combine them into one. *The Ballet of the Low Country* and *The Netherlands Ballet* now had a new name, *The National Ballet*. It was directed by Sonja Gaskell. Now The Hague had nothing. All of this was helpful for *Netherlands Dance Theater* in the end. Carel Birnie and Aart Verstegen jumped right in to take advantage of this new situation. After many meetings with The Hague officials, Carel and Aart talked them into giving us some subsidy. We also acquired the ballet studios of the former *Netherlands Ballet* after they moved to Amsterdam. Things looked promising again. There was not an endless supply of money, but our salaries improved. We could breathe again and move forward.

The Dutch television stations were very interested in dance, which in turn was good advertisement for us. They broadcasted Hans's ballet, *Judgment Party*, as well as eight additional programs that demonstrated the various types of dance, done by the different choreographers in the group. At the time, Holland had only two television stations, thus viewers mostly tuned in whether they were interested in dance or not. These television performances surely made people notice us, which meant larger audiences at our performances. We were even recognized in the streets! Hans van Manen also made a ballet for television called *Cain and Able*. In the ballet, Cain kills Abel because of a dispute over a woman. I was that woman. Part of the ballet was filmed showing Jaap and I dancing in different spots in Amsterdam, including a scene on a moving barge on a beautiful canal. Later, Hans redid the ballet for stage.

One of our appearances on the *Teddy and Henk Scholte Show*.
Bottom row: Mabel, me, and Charles Czarny.
Top row: Hans van Manen, Catarine Bottemanne, and Gerard Lemaitre.

Jaap and I in the television production of *Cain and Able*.

During this time in Holland, the *Teddy and Henk Scholte Show* was a popular monthly television program. It was the equivalent to the *Carol Burnet Show* in America. Hans van Manen was asked to choreograph dances for their programs with three girls and three boys. This meant money for the company, but it was also a lot of fun to do. However, with these being live shows, things did go wrong at times. On one occasion, they did not record our music for some unknown reason. In any case, those fingers that had to put the needle on the record must have been very shaky because it landed on the wrong place. It was a good thing the six of us were professional enough and performed the best we could under the circumstances. When the dance was finished, Hans was infuriated. It was his work with his name and reputation attached to it. Instead of disappearing from the camera as we had rehearsed, his anger took over. With a sullen face, he walked off in front of the live television camera for the whole country to see. He stormed into a hallway and sat so purposefully on a costume trunk that he fell right through it. At that moment, I walked into the hallway and found Hans completely pinned and doubled up in the trunk. We laughed but Hans said through gritted teeth," Help me out of here fast! If Henk or anyone from the show sees me in this funny predicament, it is impossible to be angry with them anymore."

Due to the popularity of the television programs, Hans received a much-coveted invitation to choreograph a dance for the *Catharina Valente Show* in Berlin, Germany. Catharina Valente was a world known singer who would produce her own variety shows. It was quite luxurious. The six of us flew first class, and were even invited into the cockpit. I can still recall how clear the night was and how we could see the twinkling lights of Berlin as we soared above it. It was an absolutely breathtaking site. It just so happened that Jerome Robbins *Dance U.S.A.* was performing in Berlin at the same time. We went to see them perform and afterwards we had dinner with a group of them, including the dancers Glenn

Tetley and Scott Douglas. We had no idea at that time, but a year later those two dancers joined our company.

Hans was then and still is one of the most talented choreographers in the world. Both Hans and Rudi have traveled the world, recreating their ballets for many different companies. They have become household names in the ballet world, and I am forever grateful to have been part of their beginnings as well as a dancer in their ballets. Presently, Hans and I are not as close as we were when we were young, although we do occasionally see each other. Rudi and I remained good friends until his death in 2012. Whenever Rudi came to America or Canada for work, we coordinated a visit and when he was battling cancer, we had daily conversations on the phone. He was not just a friend, he was family and I miss him terribly. In his Will he left me his self- portrait. I had admired it as long as I can remember, and now I can appreciate it every day. It was hanging in the literary museum in The Hague in Holland. When I pass away, it has to return to the museum. Besides being an accomplished choreographer, Rudi van Dantzig was a well-known writer.

TWENTY-SIX

Going To America

My personal life was at a standstill after my short-lived relationship with Liesbet's brother, and at times I felt a bit down about it. I was 23 years old and lonesome. My male friends were mostly homosexuals and had partners, and my girlfriends all had boyfriends or husbands. I knew I was the reason my romantic life was not progressing. My secret prevented me from getting close to anyone. I remember a Spanish performer who came to the studio to watch a class. I felt his eyes watching me the entire time. He was cute but the only thing I thought was, "Do not make eye contact." Hans even said while in class, "Talk to him he can't keep his eyes off you."

I felt I needed a breather, a kind of time out from the life I was living. One of the dancers had gone to New York to study with Martha Graham and told me how much she had learned from that experience. The style of ballet was changing in the company; it was very much influenced by modern dance. Martha Graham was THE most famous person in modern dance at the time, and I thought that going to New York and learning her style would give me a new fresh perspective on my life and work. These thoughts arose while sitting alone in a dressing room putting on make-up. I was anxious about proposing my new plan of New York to Carel Birnie and Hans, who had taken over Ben's Artistic Director post . The conversation went smoothly and we agreed on a ten-month stint in New York but I had to sign a contract for the season after my return. Carel helped me find the finances for my American adventure, and in the end I felt confident and excited about my decision. I had been performing for ten years, since I was fourteen years old. My whole world was ballet but now I was curious, what else was out there. I still had the remainder of the season to dance in Holland but New York was a nice carrot dangling ahead.

In the meantime, the company invited the American choreographer, John Butler, to recreate his ballet, *Carmina Burana* for us. He chose me for one of the four leading parts. Ben told him it was not a good idea because I was leaving at the end of the season, so that it would be better to take someone else. He didn't take no for an answer and I am so happy about that. Aside from Rudi's *Night Island*, it was the most exciting ballet I ever danced. I loved the story. Again, it was something I could do so much with. My partner was Glen Tetley, who was great to work with, and the music was very inspiring. Besides other ballets, I danced *Carmina* for the whole season, many times with orchestra and chorus. The ballet was a very big success and I was thrilled with the accolades I received from John. He was the sweetest man and helped me with my self-esteem. He thought I was interesting enough to have dinner with before some of the performances. No outside choreographer I had worked with had ever done that.

It is hard to tell if I would have gone to New York if John had come earlier to set this Ballet. I would love to relive that season with John Butler, but looking back, I have no regrets. After all, I would not be here writing this now if I had stayed in Holland.

Camina Burana

TWENTY-SEVEN

New York, New York, this Wonderful Town

The dancer Job Sanders, a member of our company, was going to New York to dance with his ex-wife Sonja Arova for some guest performances with American Ballet Theater. I asked him to see if anyone could use a roommate for the time I was there. Fortunately, he came back with good news. Anne, a former dancer from American Ballet Theater, had a roommate who was leaving and she invited me to stay with her. To get acquainted we wrote letters to each other. Anne seemed nice and I looked forward meeting her. She asked how we would recognize each other upon my arrival in America. For fun, I asked her to distinguish herself by putting a feather in her hat. On the day of my departure, all my colleagues from Dance Theater came to wave me farewell. This was arranged by Carel Birnie, he would do anything for free publicity. The next day the Dutch newspapers had a big article about me and a big picture of everyone waving me off.

The boat trip of six days was quite exciting because we had two days of very rough seas. There were ropes all over to hold on to otherwise it was hard to walk anywhere and many people got seasick. I actually loved it. I remember sitting in the movie theater with the ship rising and falling, and thinking how lovely it felt being cradled like a baby. The boat passed The Statue of Liberty very early in the morning and that was a very special moment.

Anne and I.

When we docked in Hoboken, there was a petite blonde girl with a feather in her hat. We had a laugh about the feather, which immediately broke the ice. Anne had a lovely face and personality to match it. She had stopped dancing a couple of years prior and was now working as a secretary in a small company. She was smart and good at her job. Anne was born and raised in Queens, New York and although we came from very different backgrounds, we got along from the very start.

It was 1963 when I arrived in New York. Anne's apartment was on 66th Street close to the corner of Central Park West. My first day in the Big Apple was full of new experiences and sights; Times Square was the first of many. I was fascinated and in awe over the skyscrapers, the beautiful park and the tremendous hustle and bustle of not only the street traffic but the sidewalks as well. It felt like the whole city was vibrating. We passed Howard Johnson's Ice-Cream Shop, and I could not believe how many flavors of ice cream they offered. Everything in America was so new. With every turn I was confronted with something that amazed me. American people astonished me the most. I found them to be more open, very easygoing and less uptight than the Dutch. I am not talking about my dancer friends in Holland, just people in general. Americans seemed genuinely interested in people's lives, and they asked questions to learn about each other, a quality I loved. In Holland this would be considered somewhat nosy. One thing was very clear to me, Americans were spoiled in many ways and didn't realize how privileged they were in comparison to Europeans at that time.

Anne's parents lived in Flushing, New York. They welcomed me as if I was part of the family. They were the sweetest people. I was always welcome in their home and so were their friends who were mostly neighbors. Many weekends Anne and I would venture to her parent's home and marathon watch old Betty Davis movies until the wee hours of the morning. This was such a treat since we didn't have a TV in our apartment. During this time I got to know Anne's family very well and came to understand more of their ethnological make up. I was surprised by how Anne's parents raised their ten year old son. He was babied so much and as a result unable to stand on his own two feet. Life was surely much different here than in Holland, or maybe I compared it too much with my own life and upbringing.

When I came to Martha Graham's school, her company happened to be performing in Holland. While there, *The Martha Graham Company* got together with my colleges and told Ms. Graham that I was taking classes at her school in New York. When the company returned home, Martha Graham entered her studio while we were in the middle of a class and called me by name to give a correction. I thought how does she know me? Apparently, my Dutch friends had told her she could recognize me by looking at my feet. In addition to taking classes with Martha Graham, I planned to take some jazz classes but decided to do some ballet classes instead. When I arrived at the school to take my class, I got on the elevator with Maria Talchief, the prima ballerina from *American Ballet Theater*. I realized we were going to be in the same class. I got personal corrections from our teacher, something all dancers like, because it shows that the teacher is interested in you. I had a scholarship at the Graham school, so I mostly did all my classes there. That is what I came for in the first place. The other classes I had to pay for so I put myself on a strict budget.

The rent for the back basement apartment in the brownstone where Anne and I lived was seventy dollars a month, and our electricity and telephone were relatively cheap. The apartment consisted of a big room with our two single beds on one wall and a table in between. The rest of the room had a big closet, a couple of cozy club chairs with a cocktail table that faced a fireplace that didn't work. The kitchen was big enough for two to eat in, and behind that a full bathroom. The highlight of the apartment was the terrace that we entered via the kitchen. We loved tanning and would drench ourselves with peanut oil and use foil reflectors to get as brown as possible. There was nothing wrong with doing that at that time. I was smoking too because no one knew it could give you cancer.

In the wee hours of the morning, we awoke to the police banging on our apartment door. They wanted to get to our terrace to look around. A murder had taken place in one of the houses on our street and they were searching for the murderer. This news frightened us to the core since our door had been open all night to let in the cool night air. If someone had come in, we would not have heard it because we had a fan standing in that open doorway. It definitely was not open any longer that hot summer. Unfortunately, air conditioning on our meager budget was out of the question.

I found things in the states to be very reasonable price wise. After class, I loved going to the coffee shop around the corner from Martha Graham's studio, indulging in a delicious toasted bran muffin and a lemon coke. All of that would set me back only forty-five cents and that included a five cents tip. Coffee was a light shade of brown water in New York coffee shops at the time and for me, not drinkable.

I experienced my biggest revelation in America, and it had to do with my secret. The people in America asked me questions about the war but no one asked me about the N.S.B. In Holland the NSBers and the Germans were thought of as equally iniquitous in the war. The song that my mother had forbidden me to sing, "Away with the krauts and the NSB," tells it all. My American circle of friends had not personally experienced the war, and therefore were far removed from what occurred in Europe. I realized that no one in my circle of friends knew anything about the N.S.B. My guilty burden felt as far away as Holland was geographically. A feeling of freedom consumed me, one I had not felt before. I could finally live like a normal person although I knew deep down the secret would always be there. I thought why do I have to tell the person I want to marry about the N.S.B if he doesn't even know about them? I had been hiding it from everyone, so why not him too? I was thrilled not to have this heavy secret weighing me down as much in America.

I saw John Butler quite often. He had the most wonderful apartment in the middle of Manhattan, and it even had a dance studio. There were many windows displaying city views that left you breathless. On New Year's Eve, we saw the infamous ball come down in Times Square right from his studio windows. John was working on a dance for a CBS program and asked me to join. It was for a small group of dancers. One of them was Carmen De Lafallade. She and I had danced the same part in John's *Carmina Burana*. I was excited to meet her because I had heard a lot about her from John when I worked on his ballet in Holland. As the only ballet dancer of the group, I led the barre warm-up every morning. I loved dancing John's work and was terribly disappointed that I was not able to work in America because I didn't have the right papers. Sure, extra money would have been wonderful at the time but what affected me the most was missing out on the experience.

There were a couple of Dutch girls taking classes at Graham, and they were in the country permanently. One girl, Betty de Young, was dancing with Paul Taylor and another girl Marianne Monnikendam had done a couple of performances with the *Limon Company* but was now just taking classes. I became friends with both of them and would sometimes go to see rehearsals at the Paul Taylor studio with Betty. My roommate, Anne (or Anna Banana as I called her) was my best friend and we did most things together. She was my rock, and was always there whenever I needed anything. Marianne introduced me to her Dutch friend Wilhelmina, who was not a dancer but she and Marianne became my lifelong friends. All three of us were tall, lean and both of them beautiful.

From left to right, me, Willemien, and Marianne, later in life.

Things had changed for me because I was less anxious about my secret. I wasn't afraid to meet men anymore, and I had no problem getting dates. It was about time, since I was now twenty-four. I always thought I was not very good looking and skinny on top of that. This idea came from a time when my parents had a friend who was in charge of a military home. This friend asked my parents to take her job over for a year and they did. This Military Home was in the city of Amersfoort and I would visit my parents there on some weekends. My parents organized all kind of things for the soldiers to do and one was dancing socials. On one of those weekend evenings, my parents asked some young nurses to come to the dance and I happened to be there with my dancer friends Olga Dzialiner and Gaby. Mom had a hard time but finally talked us into joining the dance party as well. I stood with the other girls on one side of the room when the music started and the boys came over to ask the girls for a dance. You guessed it, no one asked me and I quietly disappeared never to return. I probably would not have wanted to dance with me either. It wasn't my looks, it was my attitude towards my secret that scared any suitors away.

Now when I thought a guy was cute, I just had to look his way and bingo. I couldn't believe it. Anne had a boyfriend who played in the American Ballet Theater orchestra and I met some guys through him. Marianne and I would double date and I had fun with this for the first time in my life. My love life did a complete one eighty, from rarely dating to getting a marriage proposal after only three or four dates with someone I had met in the street of all places. I still had good sense and was flattered, but marrying that quickly to someone who was more of a friend was not going to happen.

TWENTY-EIGHT

Hello and Goodbye

The classes at Graham were very intense and I found them hard on my back. At first it was bearable, but gradually the pain worsened and at the end of my stay I was in bad shape. Since I did not have medical insurance I had to wait until I got back to Holland to see a doctor. Before I left New York, I met a man named Paul that I was very fond of. We were having a great time together and I became more interested with him with each date. My life felt like it had turned upside down. I was torn between leaving Paul and returning home, but at the same time I wanted my back better. He promised he would come to visit me, which eased the pain of leaving him as well as something to look forward to. When I arrived back in Holland, the doctor took x-rays and discovered a slipped disk in my lower back. I needed to rest and have massages three times a week.

So there I was at my parent's house in Amsterdam again. Those horrible thoughts about the N.S.B. came flooding back into my life again and hung dark clouds over me. Anxious for my back to recover so I could dance away those dark clouds and forget again. After a couple of months, Paul visited me and my back improved little by little. Paul and I had a wonderful romantic time together. We did go out with Hans and Gerard and had dinner with my parents. It ended with three days in Paris before he was going back to America. Things at home looked the same, but did not quite feel the same. I didn't enjoy my life in Holland anymore.

I missed Paul, but in retrospect, I think I missed America even more. I was toying with the idea of going to live in America after my stay there, but when Paul asked me to come back, it helped me with the decision. I thought hard if this was what I really wanted. I would have to say goodbye to everything I had worked so hard for so many years. I had tasted the freedom in America and that was the main drive in my decision more than Paul or anything else. I wanted to be free and happy again.

I adored my new American friends and the way of life in New York. I didn't have a job lined up, but thought I would worry about that when I got there. This was a huge step but I was young and was ready to make the move. What happens, happens. In other words, if we freeze to death, we freeze to death.

There it was again that strange expression, "If we freeze to death, we freeze to death," an expression that has a history which I will explain. At the time when Rudi, Toer and I were a close bunch, I used that expression often and jokingly. It became "Hannie's expression" but was now for fun used by them for every little decision that had to be made. For instance, shall we eat pie or cake? Let's eat cake, if we freeze to death, we freeze to death. Years later Rudi wrote a play and told me that he had used the expression in it. I don't know how he used it, but after the opening night he called and told me it had gotten a laugh from the audience. Toer and I still say it occasionally but I use it in here as a sweet memory of my dear friend Rudi.

Anne's parents generously offered to sponsor me. However, her parents did not have enough income to qualify as a sponsor. Therefore, I had to have an interview at the American embassy with the ambassador. The ambassador wanted to find out what kind of work I was going to do in America so I would not become a liability for the country. I told him that I was hoping to dance. Luckily, the ambassador knew me. He had seen me dance on stage and on television and I believe that helped me to get the papers for a green card. At the end of the dance season, I said goodbye to that chapter of my life and left Holland.

TWENTY-NINE

A Surprise Meeting

All my belongings, including my toe shoes, were neatly packed in a travel trunk Papa found at the Amsterdam flea market. It was shipped by boat and paid for by the Dutch government, a courtesy for all who emigrated. I liked this perk, but it also gave me the feeling of the Dutch saying "good riddance." For this trip to America, I traveled by plane instead of boat. While I was getting settled in my seat, a flight attendant approached and handed me a small package. This mysterious parcel was from Hans and Gerard. My two beloved friends had come to see me off but arrived too late. Tears softly rolled down my cheeks when I opened the parcel and saw a small golden heart. I was so touched by their kindness and thoughtfulness. To this day, I still treasure that golden heart. Sitting on the plane with the heart in my palm, tears began to flow harder but for other reasons. My two friends had gone to such lengths in seeing me off and making me feel so special, but at the same time this accentuated the sadness I felt about my own parents. They didn't come to see me off. They gave me two hundred dollars to start my new life, though, and I was grateful for that. Later Mom told me that she had to talk Papa into giving that money to me. What is the matter with her?

During the last few months in Holland, letters from the man who I was thinking of marrying had lessened to the point that I questioned him. His retort was that he was too busy to write.

Upon arriving in New York I came to find out he certainly was busy, he was married! Needless to say I was shocked at first but feel like I recovered quickly since I had always held back some of my feelings in self-protection. However, I was in America now, the place where I wanted to be so I wasn't going to let that nasty affair bring me down. In addition, there was enough going on at Anne's parent's house where I was staying.

While I was back in Holland, Anne had fallen in love with the man of her dreams and was engaged to be married. I was to be her maid of honor and everything was in full swing for the big event. This joyous celebration for my friend certainly kept me busy and helped me getting over the Paul affair.

Anne's talented mother made her wedding dress as well as a dress for me, plus all the specialty things related to weddings. Her wedding was beautiful, it left me awe stuck and impressed. Everything was so different from a wedding in Holland at that time. Typically, a wedding in Holland consisted of a short ceremony at the justice of the peace, followed by a dinner with the parents and the couple's best friends who were their witnesses. Now after living in the United States for many years, I know I did not perform all the customary maid of honor duties for Anne's special day. At that time, I had no idea of what I should be doing and my dear friend was too sweet and kind to complain.

After the wedding, I stayed at Anne's parent's house a little longer and found a job at the World's Fair, located that year in New York close to their home. At that time there were World's Fairs, hosted by different countries just like the Olympics. Many countries got together and promoted themselves at those fairs by showing all the wonderful qualities their country had to offer. The giant globe that still stands in Flushing is a memento from this World's Fair.

I worked in one of the shops and happened to meet a customer, who little did I know at first meeting would be a big part of my life. We started talking and I saw that he was interested in me. Although somewhat older than me, he looked nice. After talking a bit with this fellow named Frank, he asked me to join him for lunch. I was done with work anyway so I thought why not. We talked for hours during lunch and I found myself to be comfortable with him. From that day on, we shared many lunches together. Frank was fourteen years my senior, and I questioned if that was okay. I had never dated someone that old. Frank did not look his age. He was actually quite handsome, tall with medium brown hair and a radiant smile that melted my heart. Beside his good looks, Frank treated me like royalty, something his younger counterparts did not do. Not only was he generous, but a pleasure to spend time with. For once, I felt completely myself and comfortable. The more time we spent together, the more my feelings grew. I was definitely falling in love.

My life in the states was coming together and I was happily content. I had moved to Manhattan and was rooming with a friend of Anne's parents. She was a small, heavyset Jewish woman nicknamed Chippy. When she was a little girl, her family started calling her by that name and it stuck for the rest of her life. My name changed too. In Holland everyone called me Hannie, which is my calling name for Johanna. When I came to America and told men my name, some men joked with me by saying, "Can I call you darling." It got to me, if Hannie sounds too much like honey to them I would rather they call me Johanna.

Chippy was a financially stable widow who was too social to sit home every day. She worked part time, but only as long as it did not interfere with her beloved afternoon soap operas. Her kitchen always had little packages of sugar, mayonnaise, ketchup, and salt and pepper. She pilfered them from diners and coffee shops thus she never bought these items in a grocery store. Chippy was full of advice; not only did she promote her packet embezzlement but she also always advised me to let a man take care of me. When I needed a winter coat the first year in America, Chippy advised me to ask Frank to take care of it. I was low on funds and cold that winter. I was desperate enough to asked Frank, although I didn't feel very good about it. I Remember thinking Chippy was right because Frank was happy to take me to the store and buy me a beautiful coat. I often heard Chippy's little pieces of advice running through my head that first year in NYC.

Chippy, a Manhattanite her whole life, knew many people. This meant more job opportunities for me, something I needed badly after the World's Fair closed. With her help, I got my next endeavor in the working world of New York City. I got a job as hatcheck girl at a famous restaurant called The Trader Fix, located opposite The Plaza Hotel. The hours were perfect because it kept my days free for ballet classes. I was able to secure a job for my Dutch friend Willemien as well, once I heard they needed one more person.

Willemien and I shared many funny memories working together. Besides us, another girl was a veteran at the restaurant. She knew the ins and outs and taught us how to finagle the most money with a few little tricks. As a tough New Yorker, you always wanted to be on her good side. The three of us were not alone taking care of the coat check. There was a watchman to oversee all the money that transpired between the customers and us, and all the tips were supposed to go into a locked box. This included extra tips we acquired. Payment was twenty-five cents per coat, so on the end of the evening there had to be as many quarters in the box as tickets given out. Many people gave us much more than that, so when we received a dollar or more we let a quarter fall in the box and pocketed the rest. Willemien and I had a secret advantage to the system since we spoke Dutch. We let each other know the whereabouts of the watchman, so that even if we got paper money, we could let a quarter go "click" in the box. Strategically, we involved the watchman in many conversations in the back so he couldn't see what was happening in the front. When a large party arrived, we gave them one ticket and said that we put all their coats on the lower rack, which in actuality meant the floor. Sometimes the floor was full of fur coats! The watchman was fine with this because he thought that meant more money for our boss, who was his brother-in-law. What he didn't realize was that because of our little tricks it was only very profitable for us. We let one quarter fall in the pot for the whole bunch. I think his brother-in-law gave the watchman that lousy job because he needed an income and was not very smart.

The Trader Fix was an expensive, upscale restaurant, with wealthy, generous customers. Many famous people dined there, which the watchman would inform us about once we checked their coats. Willemien and I were not impressed since we had never heard of most of them. They surely were not famous in Holland. One movie star we did know was Ava Gardner! I had seen her in movies. I could smell a wonderful perfume on her coat and couldn't keep my eyes off of her because she was stunning. She was in a conversation with someone so a companion gave me her coat. Sadly, I didn't have personal contact with Ms. Gardner, something I really would have liked.

Coat check only paid $2.25 an hour, so our weekly salary did not go very far. The job would not have been worthwhile unless we did what we did. Since we were all helping each other out, at the close of the evening, we would split the money in our pockets evenly. Sometimes I went home with over thirty or forty dollars! At the time that was a good amount of money. Another benefit of working at the restaurant, we could eat in the kitchen during our breaks. The chef became a friend, and he always took care of us. Not to mention the food was spectacular. There was a soup that tasted sweet, sour and somewhat spicy and was greenish in color. I would have that every time with my dinner. We ate what the chef told one of the cooks to make for us and it was always different but delicious.

Modeling

I did for a short while try to do some modeling work as well. I am sure it is not always like that in that business but for me it was a disaster. One photographer put some music on and made me undress to half naked. He said he wanted sexy photographs for his portfolio and I needed them too for getting work, although sexy was not what I had in mind. After a while his hands were all over me to get the so called right shots. I told him that what he had on his mind was not for me. I got dressed, left that studio and walked away from modeling.

Even with that I had a great time living in this regular world for the first time. I saw Frank most days and my feelings became stronger for him. I lived life to the fullest in a wonderful city with people I cared about. My new life in New York City was coming together and I was enjoying every moment.

I paid Chippy fifteen dollars a week for rent and I had to pay for the ballet classes that I was thinking about taking again. As far as dancing was concerned I had not done anything. It had not even been very important to me. Too much had been going on from the moment I got back to New York. I lived cheaply at Chippy's, which was great for my bank account but meant sleeping on a living room couch with absolutely no privacy. If she had company, I had to be out and hope they were gone by the time I returned so the couch they were sitting on could be my bed again. Luckily, I found a furnished studio apartment on West 88th Street. The rent was twenty dollars a month more than what I had to pay to Chippy. It had a small kitchen where I now had my little packages of sugar and mayonnaise. The bathroom I shared with other people that lived on the floor. Even so, my new apartment was luxury to me; I never had it this good. However, I wasn't there often because I stayed at Frank's apartment more and more.

All my barriers crumbled and I let myself completely fall in love. Frank loved me too, and for the first time I was completely happy in a relationship. I met his parents, the children from his former marriage, and all of his friends. Frank had been married two times and had five children from those marriages. I had some concerns about Frank, not to mention his five children were a bit overwhelming as well. Two qualities that bothered me were how overly friendly he was with women at parties, and that he drank a lot. I wasn't accustomed to drinking when I was dancing and didn't know if drinking alcohol every day was a normal thing for non-dancers. I was young and thought these things were minor. I could not be happier. Frank had me wrapped around his finger, I was on cloud nine.

I started taking classes again at the Joffrey School and it felt good. Glen Tetley had come back to New York and wanted to start working on a program to perform in City Center. He asked me if I wanted to work with him. Of course I said yes. After a couple of weeks, we stopped working because he did not have enough funds for the project. I stopped taking classes for a while too because I thought there was no point. I didn't want to be in a big ballet company anymore anyway.

Frank lived in a 18th floor penthouse on Fifth Avenue. It had a large terrace which together we transformed into a luscious garden. He build the plant boxes and wired the lighting. I did all the planting and tended to the garden. When the weather was warm, the terrace was great for parties, which I took care of as well. Frank hosted parties quite often and I loved making them fun with many delectable goodies to enjoy. I was almost never at my own apartment anymore. He told me to organize the kitchen cabinets the way I wanted them and to make the apartment to my liking. My life was completely interwoven with his and I was very happy with my life as a non-dancer.

THIRTY

The Letter

I received a letter from my Mom with sad news; Papa had bone cancer. The doctors told her he only had about eight months to live. This might sound selfish, but this could not have come at a worse time in my life. My life in America was just starting to come together and then this terrible news hit me. I felt so bad, I had never seen Papa sick. He was the strongest man I knew. I had said goodbye to Holland not knowing I would return under dire circumstances a year later. I left as soon as I got the news in order to maximize my time with Papa. Frank was kind enough to buy me a plane ticket, and back to Holland I went.

Upon my arrival to our canal house on the Singel, I entered my parent's bedroom and saw my beloved Papa so weak and thin. He hardly ate and when he did, he had a hard time lifting his fork. It was heart breaking to see my strong Papa this way. Knowing things were only going to deteriorate was unbearable. He did not know he had cancer. Mom had decided not to tell him because she said it would upset him too much. I went along with it, but disagreed with her decision completely. Thus it made it that much harder and disturbing to hear my Papa say, "I will try to get out of bed, and sit a couple of minutes longer every day, so I can get stronger. Remaining in bed makes me weaker and weaker instead of better." I was very upset with Mom for keeping him in the dark about his illness. I felt he was entitled to know that his life was ending. Maybe there were things he still wanted to do while he had the time and strength. I feel bad saying this, but that is exactly the reason why I think my Mom did not want him to know. Mom had told me before I left for New York, that she thought Papa had a relation with a woman and fathered a son. When I questioned this, my mother replied that Papa had showed her a picture in the newspaper of a little boy and apparently spoke about him incessantly. She said it was as if he knew him personally. It was this ridiculous story that convinced Mom that Papa was this boy's father. For whatever reason, she never trusted him.

During this difficult time home in Holland, I began to worry about myself as well. I didn't feel sick, but I had not gotten my period for five months. My focus for the past five months had been on Papa so my own health was not at the forefront. I had gone off the pill because I developed a blood clot from them in my groin. I was instructed never to take them again. Frank and I had been very careful so I would not get pregnant. I told my mother and she suggested to see the family doctor, whom I knew well. The doctor felt my tummy and said, "First empty your bladder because it is very full." I told the doctor that I just went and right then we both knew. She did a test that confirmed my thoughts. Here I was in a place I didn't want to be, Papa dying, and me five months pregnant; what else could go wrong! The first thing I had to do was to let Frank know. Hopefully, he would make me feel better. Unfortunately, that didn't happen. Instead, he suggested I find someone to perform an abortion. Abortions were illegal in Holland at the time and besides, it was too upsetting for me even to consider. What was most upsetting that Frank wanted that option. I knew we loved each other and everything would work out in the end. I was just as surprised learning about my pregnancy as Frank was, so I was giving him the benefit of the doubt with his reaction to our news. Plus, all of our communication was through letters since phone calls were very costly. A letter would take a week to get there and then another week to get an answer back. It felt like a lifetime waiting for those letters.

My Mom was very happy about the news. I decided not to tell Papa. By now it had become clear to him that he was dying, I didn't want Papa to worry about me. Besides, he would never see his grandchild and that alone would be upsetting. Although Papa had never met Frank, he had spoken to him and thought he was a wonderful man. He was happy for me to have found someone I cared for. Papa would remark to me, "You being so far away, Frank must be missing his woman." I didn't want to pop his bubble and tell him that things were not as rosy as they seemed.

I never felt closer to Papa than I did at the end of his life. Mom was out and he had soiled himself because he was too weak to control it. Normally Mom helped him, but now I had to be the one. He cried and was upset because he felt so bad that his daughter had to clean him, and I cried with him because I felt bad that he thought that way. I would have done anything for him. The only thing I could do was to hold him and tell him that I was glad to be able to take care of him. At that time, he said, "Goodbye, my Pucky," to me. We were somber and cried, but were also at peace.

My half-sister Leny came to see Papa. They had not seen each other for many years. The reason for her absence was because she was a lesbian. When I was sixteen and moved to The Hague, Mom advised me not to look her up. When I questioned my mother, she said that Leny was hanging out with strange people and lived on top of a pub. I was young and innocent so that scared me a little. I kept my distance from Leny while living in The Hague and she never contacted me. Now with Papa on his deathbed, Leny must have wanted to make things right between them. I don't know what the discussion was between her and Papa but everything was fine between them after that. A day later Leny and I went to the store to get something for dinner, as well as bananas for my pregnancy craving. In our absence, Papa passed away with Mom at his side. It was almost as if I had not taken a breath for months and now that Papa's breathing had stopped, I was able to breathe again. His suffering was over. The most memorable thing for me happened while we were driving to his resting place. A young boy in a Boy Scout uniform saw the hearse coming and stood at military attention, saluting as Papa went by. To this day, I can still hear the sound of our footsteps on the gravel while six men carried Papa's coffin into the auditorium. That sound, still resonates within me. My Papa was gone and I missed him terribly.

THIRTY-ONE

─────────── ✧ ───────────

Happier Days Ahead

After Papa's funeral, things got better with Frank. He didn't talk about abortion any longer; we were now discussing marriage. I was full of mixed emotions. Sad because I had not planned on getting married this way but at the same time elated because I was marrying the man I loved. Not to mention anxious and hopeful that everything would turn out all right. Deep down I had some gnawing doubts about my future with Frank after everything he had said, but I pushed them away every time they surfaced. My focus was the wedding and our baby.

Frank planned on coming to Holland so we could get married. He intended to stay in Amsterdam for a little while and then return to America, while I would stay in Holland to have the baby. He said, "That way I have some time to tell my parents." They were still in the dark about everything. He adored his mother and probably was afraid my pregnancy would upset her. While I understood this, I also questioned why he was delaying the inevitable. Certainly, I would miss Frank once he returned to the states after our wedding. We would also miss sharing the birth of our child if I stayed behind, but this is what he wanted. The only positive was helping my mom look forward to something during her time of grieving Papa. Our plan changed when I found out that we couldn't marry in Holland, because both partners had to be residents of Holland for many months. I searched for an alternative and found we could get married in

England. Only one of the partners had to live there for two weeks. Off to London I went.

Gaby's mom, Phyllis, had friends living in London and they made a hotel reservation for me. They were the longest and loneliness two weeks of my life. The hotel was budget friendly to the point that heat was not included; you had to deposit money into a slot to get warmth from a small heater. I literally had to sit on top of the small heater to get any relief from the damp cold. Many times, I ran out of coins and crawled deep under the blankets to stay warm at night. The only good thing about my hotel stay was the wonderful English breakfast with all its bells and whistles. That breakfast room was always toasty warm and inviting, I looked forward to that feast every morning. It kept my stomach full until dinnertime, which was good because I didn't have much money. The money I had saved while working in New York was almost gone, so I was cautious with my spending. Frank would take care of the hotel bill when he arrived.

Under the circumstances, I didn't feel much like doing touristy things. I had just lost Papa, so sadness, and grief still overwhelmed me. I had seen the important sights of London some years before. Gaby worked there for a while as a nanny and I had paid her a visit. Too bad she wasn't here now; I would have loved her company. This London stay I mainly walked the city. I popped into stores to get warm and revisited I think one museum. I even went to some stupid movies, including a teenybopper Beach Boy movie just to be warm and get some rest. My days seemed endless, which I guess happens when you have nowhere to go.

I was in a holding period, waiting for the next steps that would determine my future. Every evening I had dinner at the same small Italian restaurant near the hotel. The food was good and in large portions. The restaurant had a typical Italian atmosphere with Chianti bottle centerpieces overrun with candle wax and purple plastic grapevines dangling here and there from the ceiling. The waiters were very kind and made me feel comfortable dining by myself. They made conversation with me, and after a couple of evenings I no longer felt like a stranger. The only people I spoke to were my restaurant friends and the people in the hotel.

Before Frank arrived in London, I spent a nice evening with two of Phyllis's guy friends. They were a couple and had graciously invited me to their home for a delicious home-cooked meal. Their home was warm, cozy and tastefully decorated. With a glass of expensive red wine in hand and easy, free flowing conversation, the evening was most enjoyable. At that time, it was okay to have a drink and even smoke while you were pregnant. I was not a big drinker but I did smoke. Thankfully, the one thing in my life that was easy was my pregnancy. I never had morning sickness or discomfort of any kind the whole nine month, but I lost a lot of hair. Maybe this was due to my very strong banana craving which I gave into and ate many. Is it possible that an abundance of potassium in your diet causes hair loss?

Frank and I had been apart for a long time now, and I counted the days until we would be in London together. All of our pregnancy and marriage conversations were done by letters and an occasional phone call. I was at the point where I convinced myself that everything was going to be fine once we were married and back living together in New York City again. The day finally came! Frank was in London and my endless loneliness subsided. Everything was as good as expected. My friends at the Italian restaurant even made us a special dinner. I was truly happy that evening sitting beside my future husband.

The next morning we left the hotel for our wedding appointment at the Justice of the Peace. When we arrived, paparazzi were waiting for us snapping photographs. I needed that like a hole in the head. The photographer had done his homework and found out I danced with *Netherlands Dance Theater*. He thought he would get some news out of it for the Dutch newspapers and wanted to talk to me. I told him I was not dancing with them anymore and he understood when he looked at my belly. He did send me the picture, but I threw it away some years later. It was the most unromantic marriage ceremony anyone could imagine. Our witnesses were a couple of strangers who were hanging around the building and didn't mind signing their names in exchange for a couple of English pounds. I even went to the extent of cracking a sarcastic joke about our nuptials saying, "Not many people in America had the opportunity to start their married life this lovely way."

After the ceremony, as a kind of afterthought, Frank asked me if I wanted a wedding band. Yes, of course I wanted one! We went into a little store that had all kinds of beautiful rings. A wide 22-carat gold wedding band immediately caught my eye. I loved it. I don't know how much it cost and to tell you the truth I didn't care. With this ring, I thee wed. I cannot remember doing anything special to celebrate the occasion other than getting ready for our flight back to The Netherlands. I was very happy that the waiting time for Frank was over, but how everything went with the wedding in London was sad. My wedding definitely was not how I had envisioned it. At least Frank was saying he was looking forward to meeting my mother and doing some sightseeing in my city, which was promising and uplifting.

THIRTY-TWO

Seeing Red in Amsterdam

Frank was as sweet to my Mother as he had been to me before I got pregnant. In her company he was nice to me too, but when we were alone he would say, "It is entirely your fault that you got pregnant." Between a diaphragm and a condom, something went wrong and I was to blame. The horrible part was I began questioning myself. Frank declared that I should have known when not to make love. In my defense, if he knew so well then why was I pregnant? It all came down to this; he was innocent, I was guilty, and I had to make it up to him. He was nice enough to do the right thing and marry me but it was understood that it had to be by his rules. Although during this time I felt his words to be very unkind, I was hopeful that he would realize this at one point. I was giving Frank the benefit of the doubt, attributing his remarks to the fact that we were finally face to face again and he was able to air his thoughts better, instead of calling and writing each other. At that time, it was not acceptable to have a baby out of wedlock. It was shameful so I was happy to marry Frank and make it right. I loved him and he said he loved me too so I was sure it would work out. I tried to be as nice to him as I could, to show him he had made a good choice marrying me. I wanted so badly for us to be happy together.

It was December 1965, a very cold winter in Holland. I took Frank to the countryside so he would get a taste of life and the scenery outside of Amsterdam. There I had the most beautiful and ugly experience. The whole winter scene was picturesque and pure, teenagers ice-skating on wooden old fashion skates in Dutch costumes of their town. The girls in their long heavy black skirts with tailored black tops and caps on their heads. The boys in their heavy black pants and matching black tops. The sky was a magnificent pink from the setting sun while everything else was white from a little fallen snow around the small lake. On the other side of the lake stood an old farmhouse with a thatched roof and a little light was coming through two of the windows. The scene in its entirety was so spectacular I felt as if I was admiring a seventeen century Dutch painting that had come to life. The serenity was quickly torn away when I overheard the crude way those teenage children spoke to each other. We had been speaking English so I am sure they felt safe speaking Dutch to one another not thinking that we would understand. I didn't translate it for Frank and spoil the scene, it would have made Holland look ugly to him and I didn't want that. It was bad enough that it made me upset.

Our site seeing included walking on the lovely canals of Amsterdam, and visiting the famous red light district. Frank was delighted seeing all those whores; one in particular caught his eye. He was flirting with her with me by his side. She was laughing and flirting back at him in her skimpy outfit. I could not believe he was doing something so hurtful to me. I was relieved when we finally left the area. A few moments later, he stopped me and said, "I hope you don't mind, but I would like to go back to that girl". Exasperated, I told him that I DID mind and if he went to her, not to touch me. With a smile on his face, Frank turned and left me standing shocked and incredibly hurt on the bridge. Was this what he meant by living by his rules? It felt as if a brick hit me, and I was completely numb inside. Thank goodness for the bridge railing in front of me to hold onto. I was torn between crying, screaming and running. Sometimes I look back at that moment and ask myself why I had not run and left Frank right then and there, instead I stood frozen to that bridge holding on for dear life. A glass enclosed tourist boat full of people enjoying the beautiful city sites passed below me. A few carefree tourists waved at me with broad smiles, which made me even more upset. Jealous of their normal lives, I turned my head pretending not to see them. What would their advice be if they knew I was waiting for my husband, of three days, to return after visiting with a whore?

It seemed like an eternity before Frank returned. He explained that all he did was talk with the whore and nothing happened between them. I wanted more than anything to believe him, but it was killing me inside. He wanted to hold my hand but I refused because I did not know what his hand had touched. I was in disbelief that Frank could be so cruel. Later that day when we were back at Mom's house the radio played a love song. Listening to it made me very upset and I walked out of the room. I wanted to live that love song but in reality, I knew I was far from it. All of the things I went through the last couple of months came to a boiling point at that moment. Mom came into the kitchen, where I was splashing water on my face and asked what was wrong. I didn't want to tell her the whore story so I said that I was tired and needed some time alone. Frank was a little nicer to me after that.

Instead of trudging through the cold on foot, we decided to take a bus tour for the day. The tour guide recognized me from dancing, which embarrassed me for reasons I could not explain very well, not because I was pregnant but more because on the outside my life appeared so normal and happy. However, on the inside it was all a sham. I had even stopped seeing my old dancer friends. Matter of fact, they didn't even know I was back in Holland. The only friend I still had contact with was Phyllis. She was a lifesaver for me when Frank was there because she spoke fluent English. I didn't have to translate everything as I had to do for my mother or Rie and her new husband Frits who lived downstairs. Frank liked Phyllis; he had a nice time when she was around which made me feel comfortable. After two weeks, it was time for him to return home and I guess it was time to tell his parents about everything. I never heard from them but Frank told me that his parents were fine with it.

THIRTY-THREE

Motherhood

When I was six months pregnant, I started calling hospitals to see if they had an opening to deliver my baby. A couple of them had no room. I felt like Mary who had no place to deliver her baby Jesus and hoped I didn't have to deliver in a stall. Thank goodness the Juliana Hospital had availability so from that point on I had all my scheduled checkups there until the delivery.

With my due date of February 21st a few months away, I had plenty of time to gather baby essentials before the birth. At that time there was no way of knowing the gender of an unborn child so I got everything white, a color I liked for a little baby anyway. I stayed with my mother and together we anxiously awaited the big event. Finally, fourteen days later than expected, labor began. Between the contractions I slept sporadically. Mom and I played cards for hours, since it was the only thing that kept my mind off the pain. After twenty-one hours of torture at home, we finally went to the hospital. Two hours later, I delivered my baby at one o'clock in the morning.

The birth would have been a day earlier if it had been taken place in New York but because of the time difference it was on March 5 that I became the mother of my little baby boy. Frank had wanted a girl, but said if it was a boy his name should be Brian, so Brian it was. Of course, he needed a middle name so I decided to give him my father's name, Johannes. Births were natural in Holland, no pills, gas or shots. After all the pain I endured, I distinctly remember when they finally wheeled me in a room to sleep, I was beyond grateful.

One thing all American Moms would be jealous of is after I gave birth I was required to stay in the hospital for ten days. This extended stay was mainly for rest, but also to teach you to bathe, dress and nurse the baby. I stayed in a big room with about nine other young mothers. This was beneficial as well since some were not first time mothers and could give helpful advice. I nursed Brian on the times they told me and he stayed next to me in a little crib the whole day. The nurses would come in and take him away for a change but brought him right back when it was done. After our dinner and another feeding, they rolled the babies out and you could sleep until breakfast. During visiting hours when I saw how happy the dads were, I was regretful that Frank wasn't there to enjoy this special time with me. The last day in the hospital the mother had to bathe and dress the baby without help from the nurse. I thought this whole extended stay was invaluable to new mothers.

Leaving the hospital, I asked Mom if she had an alarm clock because I had to make sure I would wake up to feed Brian during the night. Well everyone who has had a baby knows what a big joke that was and I got that joke fast. My mother loved having us there; it helped both of us to get over the death of my father. We often remarked on how Papa would have loved Brian. He had wanted a son but got me, and Frank wanted a daughter and got a son. Why it is that people always do that, be happy with whatever comes your way. People make things so complicated for stupid reasons. That little boy consumed our thoughts and lives. I could not stop looking at him, he was so beautiful.

Frank asked if Brian was circumcised. It was something I had not even contemplated. In Holland, it is not automatically performed on every male baby, only if it is important to you or if you are Jewish. Our son was now two weeks old and I had to find out where this could be done. The answer was in a Jewish hospital. I walked into a big operating room and had to put my tiny little baby on a large white sheeted operating table with an enormous lamp over it. I told those bearded doctors to take it easy on him and went far enough away so I would not hear his cries. He was still sobbing when they called me back in but at least it was over.

Things were quite normal between my mom and I since we needed each other. Having us there helped Mom to cope with her grief and I needed her expert baby advice since she had been helping my half-sister Henny after the births of her three children. I had not shared my worries about my future with Frank with my mother. I felt Mom didn't care much about my feelings. While Frank was staying with us, she must have seen how he treated me even without knowing English, but she always had a big smile for him and said nothing to me. It was more than wanting to stay out of my business. It was an easy way out for her, blowing with the wind. God forbid she should stand up for something or for some-one. On the other hand, she always had negative things to say to me about her best friend Rie. She probably did the same about me to Rie. It all sounds very harsh on my part, but at that time, I was not over everything that had happened to me when I was young. I still had to deal with my secret, although I had buried it deep in-side of me. It was also Papa's fault, but somehow knowing Mom's personality, I blamed her the most. I just didn't like her. It both-ered me that I felt that way but I couldn't get past those feelings.

While I was in Holland, Frank was supposed to rearrange the apartment in preparation for Brian and me coming home. The apartment had one spacious room which had been a ballroom in the 1920's, plus a kitchen and bathroom. Something had to be done to make a small private space for Brian within that big room. After Frank returned home, I didn't hear about any progress with the apartment. I kept on asking Frank about it in my letters, but his answer was either I am working on it, or I am still waiting for the drawings from Bob Genchek, our architect friend was drawing up. His favorite answer was, "What do you think, I have to work too." I did not want to be a nuisance, so three months went by without anything happening. It came to the point that he said," Why not come here and do it yourself. Leave Brian with your mother, and pick him up when it is done". I am sure Frank did this to torture me, because he must have known how difficult it was for me to leave my little baby behind. I thought it over very carefully. There was nothing for Brian in New York, not even a crib. Frank obviously was not doing anything about the situation so it fell in my hands to make our home a home for all of us. I asked Mom if she was willing to take care of Brian while I took care of things in New York. She was thrilled to have Brian to herself for a while. Maybe she was glad not to have to deal with me for some time as well.

THIRTY-FOUR

A Twenty Dollar Joke

Back in New York, I worked diligently to get everything ready for Brian. It was not an easy task because I was missing my little boy tremendously and drying up after I stopped nursing was very painful. I tried pumping, but seeing my nipple being sucked in the pump made me very queasy and I could not continue. As for the apartment, Bob Genchek did a great job rearranging the space so Brian had his own little room with a big window that overlooked Central Park. I did enjoy seeing Frank again but questioned if he felt the same. My doubts were made clearer one evening when Frank asked me to get something out of the trunk of his car. While looking through his trunk, I noticed a big bag with all kind of woman's clothing and makeup. The bag looked like it belonged to a flight attendant from American Airlines. How lovely I thought in anger. I took the big bag to the street corner and furiously hurled it into the garbage bin.

Frank must have been hanging out with her during the time he was supposed to get Brian's room ready. No wonder he was not in a hurry with it. Realizing Frank had been playing house with another woman while I was giving birth to our son in The Netherlands was truly the icing on the cake and it made me wonder about my future. Frank was very angry when I told him what I had found and what I did with it. He gave me the bologna story that someone had forgotten the bag at his friend's house and he had offered to bring it to the person as a favor because she lived close to us. That was the reason why it was in his car. He said, "Go down and get it." Too late, it was gone. I told him that I saved him a trip bringing it back to the woman. I was shaking from hurt and anger. Why did he ask me to get something out of the trunk in the first place? Was he that stupid or did he purposely want me to find the bag and thought I would not say anything? He surely didn't count on me having the nerve to throw it away. I was happy with the way I had handled it, but it took me a very long time to get over this dirty happening. In any case, Brian's room was completed and even though I didn't know what Frank was up to in my absence, I returned to Holland to get my little boy. I told myself, everything was going to be better once we were living together as a family. I was going to make that happen.

When I saw Brian again, I was shocked at how much he had grown in my short absence. Mom had done a great job with him and I was grateful for that. Frank liked my Mother and told me she could visit us any time, which made it a little easier for her to say goodbye. When Brian's passport was ready, we flew home to New York. At the age of 5 months, my son met his father for the first time. It wasn't a special event for Frank, after all this was baby number six for him. I was proud showing Brian to Frank's friends and family and was surprised that they all bought him lovely gifts. This type of gift bearing was not done much in Holland. What made me the happiest was seeing Brian lying in his crib in his own little room. He was home.

Frank had met a girl in the elevator of our building while I was back in Holland. When he realized she was Dutch, he told her about me and she said that when I returned to New York to let her know, so we could meet. Frank told her that I was not interested in meeting other Dutch people. We did meet after all and she told me the strange remark Frank had said to her. Whatever his reason, it didn't matter, we became friends anyway whether he liked it or not.

What bothered me a little was that Frank was tight with

money. He didn't want me to work so I had to rely on him to give me money for whatever we needed. Frank made sure to give me just enough for food. However, this arrangement did not sit well with me since I had always taken care of myself and never relied on others. Nevertheless, it was what he wanted so I went along with it. His joke was, "Here is twenty dollars, don't spend it in one place ha, ha." Lucky for me, I was used to being frugal with money so that part was not a big deal. I tried very much not to spend it in one place. If I could get something cheaper five blocks away, I would go there to save some pennies and show him how good I was with his money. The funny thing was that there was enough money. Frank was vice president of his stepfather's electrical contracting firm and made a very good living. .

We entertained business people quite often in our home, which I liked to do. They were mostly older couples around Frank's age. The husbands had important jobs in big companies that could help Frank get electrical contracts for projects in and around Manhattan. He wanted to impress his friends and would go through all kinds of recipe books to find things for me to cook. I was sometimes busy for days with preparations. I didn't mind because I could see that he was always proud to show me off to those business friends and their wives. During this time, I thought to myself, see he loves me and is realizing I am a good wife. I did my best to be a good hostess and prepare the extravagant dinners he requested. I know I succeeded because everyone always had a good time, including Frank. He probably got complements from the men about me because he was always nice to me after the company left.

When the twenty dollars were gone, I had to ask for more. I hated to do this because he would question why it was already gone. Of course he didn't think I could make gourmet dinners for pennies. It was to make sure I would spend as little money as possible. All of those negatives at that time I felt I deserved, because of the pregnancy and the fact that I had been an N.S.Ber. He would not have married me if he had known that, I was convinced about that. I didn't feel good keeping him in the dark about it, but did not see another way. There was one thing I was sure of, even though I thought I had been an N.S.Ber, I could never see myself doing the things the N.S.B. was guilty of. I would have behaved the opposite if I had been an adult at that time. Of course, if I told people about my background they would not believe that. This is something I really believed at the time and even now still lingers on a little.

Our home on Fifth Avenue was really too small. We had to sleep on a pullout couch which was getting to us. It was like living at Chippies again. When we had guests, I longed for them to leave so I could go to sleep on the couch they were sitting on. I vividly remember one New Year's Eve. At 2 am the people on our couch were not moving, drunken Frank told them, "I don't know what you want to do but I want to go to my bed and you are sitting on it". I had never seen those people before and I never saw them after that incident either. They were not that important to Frank otherwise he would not have said it.

Since space was tight in our apartment, there was certainly no room for my mother when she came to visit. Thankfully, the gay couple below us said we could rent one of their bedrooms for the duration of her stay. In addition to limited space for our guests, and no private bedroom for Frank and I, there was also Brian who was getting older and in need of more space as well. His tiny room was not big enough to house a regular sized bed, so a move was inevitable. The neighbors below us bought a brownstone in downtown Manhattan. We liked their new house and planned to rent a floor from them after it was renovated. Everything would be ready the same time as our lease was up at the penthouse. Frank made a stink with Mrs. Miller our landlady about the security money she didn't want to give back to him because of the little room we made. He yelled at her and made her very upset, which turned into them not speaking to each other anymore. Unfortunately, the brownstone was far from ready to move in when our lease was almost up. Frank asked me, "Why don't you go downstairs and ask Mrs. Miller if we can extend the lease for two months?" When I spoke to her, she said she would have done it for me, but after the way Frank spoke to her she had to say no. Thus, we were forced to move out and had nowhere to go.

THIRTY-FIVE

Roaming Around

Before we vacated Fifth Avenue there was a lot of work to do. The terrace was filled with big redwood boxes overflowing with trees and plants. Frank had also installed extensive outdoor lighting and didn't want to leave anything. He felt it was increasing the value of the apartment that Mrs. Miller would take advantage of. A doctor who lived in the penthouse in the adjacent building wanted everything, so that is where it all went.

Movers put all our furniture in a room at the guy's unfinished brownstone and we moved into a hotel. Frank found us a room in a hotel in the mid-fifties between Fifth and Sixth Avenue. It was a large room with a big bed in the middle, that had heavy curtains hanging on both sides and the same curtains on the windows. Those windows looked out onto the stone wall of the next building and didn't give us much natural light. Thus, we had the golden little sconces on all the time. The curtains and the wall-to-wall carpet were a dark burgundy that gave the whole room a reddish glow. As far as I could tell, there were only some old ladies living on our floor. Sometimes a door was left open and I got a small glimpse of someone who looked like an old actress or showgirl. One door was open almost every time I passed, and typically had music from the forties or earlier pouring from it. When Brian and I approached the open room one day someone very frail with bleach blond hair was sitting in a chair and asked, "Is that you, Henry?" when she heard us coming. I informed her that we were not Henry and then had a hard time looking away from the old tenant. Her apartment reminded me of an old fascinating movie scene. Everything was in different shades of pink. The lampshade of the lamp with a table attached to it gave the room a pink glow and lots of pink ruffles adorned her chair. She was wearing a shiny long dark pink robe and had a pink ribbon tied in her hair. Although the door was always open to different degrees, I had never actually seen her before. Looking back, I wish I had walked in and spoke with her a little more as well as some of the other ladies from the hotel. At the time I felt I was intruding on their privacy, but also, and it's silly to me now, I was a little afraid of them.

Overall, the hotel was a very depressing place to live in and gave me an uneasy feeling. I couldn't entertain Frank's business friends of course, so Frank would take them out by himself for lunch or evenings without the wives. I hated this new arrangement because he would return late at night smelling of perfume. Who knows where he had been, who he touched and had fun with. The hotel had no kitchenettes so we would eat in Chinese restaurants together when Frank was not entertaining potential clients. I had brought an electric cooktop on which I prepared simple meals for Brian and myself. Brian slept in the corner of this horrible room, I felt so guilty bringing him to this hell hole. Thank goodness there is an abundance of activities for children in New York so we went elsewhere every day. Brian liked Central Park the most, so we frequented there often.

Brian was a very active three year old and I had the daily challenge keeping up with him. He was running all over the place and I was afraid of losing him. The Central Park Zoo had a children's zoo that was all enclosed with one little entrance and the exit next to it. I stayed at that exit so he could do all the running around he wanted. I was able to keep him within sight and not worry about him getting lost. He loved that place, it had a wooden boat, a castle, and other things children could climb on, and he always found a friend to do it with. On the different playgrounds on the other hand, I would get as much exercise as him. I was constantly on the run to get him when he decided to explore beyond his boundaries.

The renovation went much slower than expected and I couldn't stand being in that depressing hotel any longer. I found a different hotel in the east seventies that had a kitchenette and sometimes too much sunshine. We stayed there for the hottest summer I can remember and the place had no air conditioning. Frank would lie in a cold bath after work to cool off. He often had business lunches, and doing a lot of drinking with lunch was not the smartest thing to do in all that heat. He drank too much anyway. When you saw Frank, you would also hear the ice jingling in his vodka gimlet.

We had given up waiting for the apartment in the village. I started to look for something more permanent and found a great place in a brownstone on Sixteenth Street close to Sixth Avenue. We had to be out of the hotel at a certain time, but could not get into our new apartment for some hours. I thought it was somewhat funny to think that we were now homeless. Frank was a member of the New York Athletic Club, and there was a BBQ that day at their facility on Travers Island in Pelham. We decided to go there for those homeless hours. When it was time to leave the hotel, we loaded all of our belongings that we accumulated into Frank's car and it was packed to the brim. I had a hard time finding room in the car for Brian or myself. There were things up, down and around us. Sitting in a very uncomfortable position in the back of the car, Frank said very irritated, "I cannot see anything with all that hair." I had my hair up and for him it was my hair and not the stuff that made it hard for him to see out of the back. I had to laugh so hard tears rolled down my face. I just could not stop. He couldn't understand why I thought it was so funny. He was irritated with the situation, wanted to take it out on me, and I was laughing. How was that possible?

THIRTY-SIX

Entertaining Young and Old

I was thrilled to finally be in a home with lots of space. No more pull-out couches or hotel rooms for us, and Brian was happy to have a sunny room of his own. He was three and a half now and a handsome little boy. Brian's shape of his face and eyes he had gotten from me, but his blue eyes were from his Father. We had only spoken Dutch together his whole life. He understood English somewhat but could hardly speak it. I don't have to go into details to tell you how much time Frank had spent with his little boy, because this says it all. Brian also had very little contact with children besides the ones he met at various playgrounds. I decided he needed more exposure with children his own age and found the perfect solution with a wonderful little school at Gramercy Park. When I arrived to pick him up after his first day, he didn't want to leave. He saw that other children were staying longer and didn't want to miss out on the good time. After that first week I gave in and let him stay for full days. Brian's English improved and after a few months when I spoke Dutch to him, he would answer in English. This was a little sad for me since I wanted him to keep up with the Dutch language but saw it disappearing little by little.

I was always trying to please Frank and made sure I did everything to make him happy. It was always on my mind why he had married me. He didn't bring that up any longer but he didn't have to, I knew it all too well. I went along with all of his wishes. He had complete control over our money, and I had no idea how much was in our bank account. In fact, I didn't even think of it as our money, it was his money. I had no credit cards, nothing more than those twenty dollar bills when they came my way. When I asked for two twenty dollar bills, I had to explain why I needed so much. Entertaining was in full swing again after the move and that was my full time job.

Our new apartment was in a nice friendly neighborhood. After a while, I knew all the shop owners and even though we lived in this big city, the neighborhood had a feel of a small village. On the corner of our street was a paper stand where a homeless man was always hanging out. I had thrown an old knit dress out and the next day I saw this homeless guy wearing it, with the bottom cut off. I said to Brian," Look at mommy's old dress." It was so funny it made us both laugh. It was even funnier to me because I still had that dress from when I was living in Holland. Thinking back to the time when I had bought it, who would have thought that eventually a homeless man in New York would wear it.

On the corner of the street near Brian's school was a tavern where I used to go with Anne sometimes when we lived together. Looking at the place brought back memories of how carefree and happy that time had been. So much had happened in those few years. Was I happy to be in this country instead of living in Holland? Yes, I really loved living here, but was not very happy with my life. It was not that Frank and I fought a lot, I made sure of that. It was difficult to keep the peace, and constantly mirroring Frank's mood was tiresome. I had the tolerance to undertake all of that but not trusting his fidelity made me very unhappy. I felt inadequate as a woman. We had some good times but I am sorry to say that I created most of them.

Brian and I frequented the playground in Union Square Park almost every day after school. He played with his buddies who lived on our street, and I socialized with their mothers. There were always some drug addicts hanging around the park but they didn't bother us much. They kept to themselves except one time when one decided to have a joy ride on Brian's tricycle. I scrubbed that tricycle until the paint came off before letting Brian ride it again. I was happy for my son that he now had a nice, stable environment, after all the moving around like gypsies. This normalcy was good for us too; everything was going to be fine now.

Dancing had been on the back burner, but I mostly missed the exercising. Now that Brian was in school, I had more free time. I spoke with Frank about taking ballet classes again, and when he agreed, I went back to the Joffrey School. I could walk from my apartment to the school and then did my grocery shopping after class. We would have at least two dinner parties a week, sometimes more. I would prepare for them while Brian was in school, pick him up and then let him play a little in the park before going home. Summer was coming and school ended for Brian. For me to take my classes we needed a babysitter, and Frank was not willing to pay for that. I enjoyed my classes because it was something I did just for me. While in class my mind was off my daily routine, and that was refreshing. The true enormous desire I used to have to dance had disappeared, so it wasn't too painful to stop. I believed Frank when he said that he and Brian would miss me too much if I got too involved in dancing. I know Frank missed me when he was at work because he called me at least three times a day to hear what I was doing. This made me feel good because it proved that he loved me.

The most important people to Frank were the business associates we entertained. Some of them were his best friends. He encouraged me to get close to their wives, something that was not easy to do. Most of them lived in the suburbs, were involved in their church or the PTA, and New York City was too intimidating for them to even drive into by themselves. I didn't really have much in common with them anyway, they were mostly much older than me and were not much fun to be with. Anne and her husband had moved to Boston, so there was not too much contact with her anymore. The only good friend I had in New York was Willemien. She was a friend through thick and thin, and was always there with a listening ear.

Every other Saturday we traveled to Long Island to visit Frank's four children from his former marriage. In the winter we took them to the movies and then dinner at a Chinese restaurant, something that was not easy when Brian was an infant. In the summer it was easier; we could go to the beach or an amusement park, places that were more enjoyable for Brian as well. The children, two boys and two girls, were nice and I mostly had decent times with them. The oldest girl, Pamela, was very helpful keeping Brian entertained, but I felt very sorry for the youngest girl, Carolyn. There was definitely something wrong with her. She craved so much attention, something she obviously did not get from her mother or father. She would take my hand and put it on her face. I tried to give her as much love as possible. Frank's oldest son Lloyd was okay but the youngest Richard was a real mommy's boy who didn't really want to be there, but had to come. He always had trouble with his stomach and many times Frank had to take him out of the movie because he had to throw up. I was always exhausted after those outings, mainly from keeping Brian under control so Frank would not get upset.

The children were not especially close to Frank. I think they were the closest to their grandmother with whom they lived with their mother. I never met either one of them; they never came out of their house when Frank picked the kids up. Frank's son from his first marriage, Chris, I only saw for a little while when he needed help getting settled in Manhattan. I found him an apartment and arranged for whatever he needed to live in it and that was the last I saw of him.

THIRTY-SEVEN

My Extended Family

Frank's oldest son Lloyd came to live with us at the age of fifteen because, his mother was not able to handle him any longer. He had done poorly during the school year and needed to attend summer school. The caretaking of Lloyd became my job, a job his own mother could not do. I felt I was not well equipped to be a substitute mother for a troubled teen but had no choice. Frank didn't trust that Lloyd would attend his summer school classes if he was unsupervised. Every day I had to bring him and pick him up. He refused to walk next to me so he was always three steps in front of Brian and I. We had a hard time keeping up with him. I felt like a police woman and didn't enjoy this any more than he did. However, I was afraid that if I didn't escort Lloyd to and from school, he would not attend which meant trouble with Frank. Not only was I Lloyd's personal escort but his tutor as well. While assisting him with his homework he would sit and stare out of the window instead of listening to any of my instructions. I failed in helping Lloyd but on the other hand, I think he needed professional help. He was miserable and the whole summer school situation brought me to the end of my rope. Frank finally realized that this was not working, and something else had to be done.

Since Frank was from Irish decent, he researched and found a boarding school in Ireland for Lloyd. At the end of the summer, the four of us vacationed in Ireland before bringing Lloyd to his new school. What I remember from our trip was Frank constantly picking on Brian and telling me how I was not doing a good job with him. Don't forget this was Frank's first time ever spending any time with Brian on a daily basis. At home he hardly looked at him nor interacted with his son. I guess having done such a great job bringing up his other children he knew I was bringing Brian up all wrong.

At home when I cooked something that wasn't to Frank's liking, I would be subjected to continual criticism. But here in Ireland everything was so delicious. He loved the vegetables cooked to mush and the overcooked dry meat in a pie. It is amazing how one can love this Irish gourmet food, only because his ancestors are from there. Lloyd attended the boarding school for three years but never succeeded there either. I never saw Lloyd happy which was very unfortunate for such a young boy with so much promise in life. Sadly, he died in his early twenties in a motorcycle accident.

Frank's Mother was Irish and his stepfather was Jewish of Russian decent. Frank loved his stepfather, but he scoured the obituary section of the New York Times daily for the name of his biological father. Frank and his mother were extremely close; he called her every day, seven days a week. Frank often said that she was the best person in his life. Hearing that wasn't music to my ears, but I was still convinced that he also loved me, even if I was not his number one. His parents stayed in Palm Beach, Florida for the winter and often vacationed in Europe during the summer. They even went to Holland on one of those vacations and visited my mother on the Singel. They stayed at the Hilton located in the chicest neighborhood in Amsterdam. I was impressed because staying there for two nights would have been a month's salary when I was dancing. They said Mom made a nice dinner for them and that Phyllis joined them as well. Inviting Phyllis was smart of Mom because of the language barrier.

Frank's parents lived in a beautiful house in Kings Point,

overlooking the water of the Long Island Sound. Status was most important to Frank's mother, so everything in their house was very formal. Her housekeeper, Maddie, served us dinner and was summoned to the dining room by the chime of a little bell. During the early years of our marriage, we joined Frank's parents for Thanksgiving and Christmas dinners at their home. Needless to say, Frank's mother was excessive when it came to holidays and saw it as a chance to display her finery. We ate off French porcelain dinnerware and drank out of hand-made glasses from Venice, Italy. Everything on the table was embellished with gold designs and sparkled. I didn't care about all of this, but I could see that she loved it. I tried to picture all these settings in front of me on the little table in the houseboat where I grew up, and it made me giggle inside. Everything in their house was put together by a professional decorator, including a painting over the sofa that had to match the color scheme. I thought that was very strange, because for me you like art for what it is and not for color to enhance your furniture. Naturally I didn't tell her that; after all, to each her own.

Dad, Frank's stepfather was the sweetest man; he always made me feel comfortable. We talked about all kinds of things, like what Hebrew words were similar in the Dutch language, what my impressions were when I came to New York and his experiences when he came to America. Our conversations were always so interesting. After all, we were both immigrants, but he came to America forty five years earlier than I did. Mom did everything to make Dad comfortable, she treated him like gold. There was no doubt in my mind that they adored each other. I remember thinking to myself, if Frank and I had half of their love, I would be very happy. I loved Frank's parents and I felt they loved me in return.

Dad had started an electrical firm way back when he arrived to America. He brought his brother into the company as well and turned it into a multimillion-dollar business. He and his brother were the presidents and his brother's son and Frank were both vice presidents. Dad knew all the important business people in New York as well as the politicians, from the Governor to the Mayor and everyone else in between. He became the President of the Electrical Union and was featured on the front page of The New York Times Sunday Magazine with a big article about him.

We attended formal dinners in all of New York's finer establishments such as; The Pier, The Waldorf, and or The Plaza to name a few. At such affairs we received lavish gifts ranging from designer handbags to gold jewelry. Now I dined at the restaurant where I used to check coats when I first came to New York and I wondered if the current coat check girls had the same money system.

One of Frank's favorite restaurants was the Russian Tea Room. We frequented there so often with clients or as a couple, it felt like it was our hangout. We would also join Mom and Dad for dinners with important business people or some kind of politician and their wives. On those occasions we dined at restaurants that did not include prices on the menus. We traveled via limousine to these prestigious restaurants and were treated like royalty. From the outside it all looked like I was living a privileged life, and of course, my life was privileged in a way. I should have been happy surrounded by all that luxury, but I wasn't. Over those years The National Ballet and Netherlands Dance Theater came to perform in New York numerous times. During one of those tours, Carel Bernie of the Netherlands Dance Theater had come to our house for dinner. He noticed something rather insightful but didn't share it with me at that time. When he returned to Holland, he said to Hans van Manen, "Hannie lives in a golden cage." Years later when Hans told me that, I was surprised to learn that Carel saw that before I realized it myself.

A couple of times Frank's Mom came unannounced to the apartment to visit or bring something. I thought it was nice she thought of visiting but I wished she would give me notice. In the summer Brian and I were not always dressed by nine, or my house was not in top shape. This was especially the case after hosting a dinner party the night before. One of those mornings she brought Brian a ventriloquist doll named Charlie McCarthy from Schwartz toy store. When she gave Brian a gift, she always would say," if he doesn't like it, let me know." Well, Brian was scared to death of that doll. I had to take it out of his room at night, and felt it was a waste of money. Brian wanted some wooden trains from that store, so I thought that maybe it was possible to do an exchange. I called her, she said she understood and that ended the call.

Two hours later she called and started yelling at me, saying how ungrateful I was. At first, I thought she was joking, but quickly realized she was serious. I could not believe it; soon she was spewing more instances of where I went wrong in her eyes over the years. Awhile back, I had come to their apartment with my Mom while she was visiting us and I had remarked when my mother-in-law had steered us into the living room, "Oh we are sitting here today." She thought with that I meant, "Now that my Mother is here she allowed me to sit on the good stuff in the living room." I am sure that I meant nothing other than what I said; normally we sit in the den but not today. There was no hidden meaning or insult behind my words.

Our phone conversation had totally thrown me off guard, I felt it was so ridiculous and dumbfounded, where did this suddenly come from? My mother- in-law's accusations hurt me tremendously because I had always loved my time with my in-laws. She even had instances where I apparently offended other members of the family. For instance, I had mentioned to her sister, that I was going to buy a particular skirt when I got money for Christmas. What was wrong with that? It was true; I was waiting for the Christmas money to buy myself some things like I always did. Here I thought I was doing no wrong, being myself, living my life amongst family whom I thought enjoyed my company as much as I theirs. Apparently, in my mother-in-law's eyes, it was much different.

At this time my in-laws had just moved to Manhattan. They lived now on the corner of 57th street and Seventh Avenue. She said that they sold the house in Kings Point because I didn't want to live in the country. They had thought that we eventually were going to live in that house. All of that was news to me; no one had ever mentioned this to me. Then I had to hear, "Who do you think you are? You came from a household where you had to go down two flights of stairs to go to the bathroom." Mom had made it nice for them when they came to visit her in Amsterdam and this was what she remembered of it, how shallow was that. Knowing now her way of thinking I was glad she didn't know that I had to share a chamber pot with my parents on our tiny houseboat. Compared to that, the Singel was luxury. She also threatened that if I said anything about this conversation to Frank, she would have an earful to tell him, and said, "You better keep your mouth shut if I was you. "I told her she could tell Frank all she wanted, and I had nothing to hide. That was a big lie of course. I had my secret, but that was something I didn't think she knew, or did she? I was now somewhat worried but quickly pushed it away because if she knew my secret she would have said something about it already. It convinced me more than ever that I never should tell that secret to anyone, because eventually it would come to haunt me. She would have had a field day with it, something I didn't need. I was ashamed and guilty about that enough on my own.

I had put my mother-in-law on a pedestal, but now she came tumbling down. I told her those exact words and added how disappointing it was to realize that she thought so little of me, while I on the other hand had only warm, loving feelings towards her. I tried to defend myself but it was like talking to the wall. So the only thing I repeated again and again was how disappointed and hurt I was. She had no idea how much this was affecting me. I did tell Frank what his mother said, and he thought that it was ridiculous and to forget about it. I felt he was on my side for a change but I guess he did that so it would go away. I had embraced and loved those two people as my family and was terribly hurt by her outburst. I never felt comfortable or close with Frank's mother after that fateful phone call. How could I have been so fooled for all those years? I think my need to belong overpowered deciphering and truly seeing the qualities of the people around me.

THIRTY-EIGHT

─────── ❦ ───────

Park Avenue

When the lease of the apartment was ending, Frank decided I look for something to buy. I found an apartment on Park Avenue that needed a good amount of work, but had wonderful possibilities. Frank had not much good to say about me, but I knew he thought I had good taste. I told him all the things that could be done to make it a showplace and he agreed. The apartment belonged to an old member of the Ziegfeld Follies, who was living there with her sister who took care of her. She couldn't walk and was bed ridden. I wondered if they were going to live in that hotel with all the other old ladies after we bought their apartment. Every apartment in the building had a private storage area in the basement. After we bought the place, I realized that our storage bin had big old leather trunks full of stuff in it that the ladies had left behind. I thought I would look at all of that later; the basement was not the nicest place to be. I never got around to it and feel sorry for that, and again that I didn't talk more to the former owner. Hearing more about their lives on Broadway would have been interesting. So many things you wished you had done when you think back. I guess when you are young you just don't stand still long enough to smell the flowers.

Our architect friend, Bob, again did all the drawings for the major renovation. He was a wonderful craftsman who designed and reworked spaces in ways that I would have never thought about on my own; after all, he was an award-winning architect. The apartment needed a whole new kitchen, walls had to be removed, and all new windows installed. The old ones had little panes that I didn't like. Of course we couldn't live there during the renovation so that meant relocating again. I found us an apartment that belonged to an Indian diplomat and his French wife. They were going to India for two months and were willing to sublet their place. It was a lovely high floor apartment with an incredible view. The modern building was located a couple of blocks from the U.N. At the time, Frank was into Peking duck and wanted me to make it often. In Chinatown ducks hang in the store windows, because they are marinated and then they have to dry so that the skin gets crispy when they are cooked. I had ducks hanging in the window over the air-conditioning all the time. I imagined that neighbors who looked in thought that I had strange ideas about decorating.

To furnish our new home, Frank relied on my taste. I could buy whatever I thought looked good in it, money was no object. While I didn't have more than twenty dollars in my pocket, I went to a place in Westchester to pick out a slab of marble for some astronomical amount. This was for a five by ten foot dining table that I designed. For the living room I had couches made to the exact height and length I wanted. One little table I picked out cost more than what I could spent on my wardrobe for the year and I ordered three of them. Things were shipped from Italy, Germany and Holland. The place had three bedrooms, two baths and a very big open dining and living space, with a fireplace in the middle open to both rooms. There were ten-foot ceilings with big windows all around because the apartment sat on the corner of the building. The total space was about three thousand square feet. When it was completed, the place looked absolutely stunning. After it was finished, I changed my job from decorator back to housekeeper again.

When my Mom would come for a visit Frank always insisted she could stay for as long as she wanted. I had no say in the matter and those visits dragged out to be a couple of months. He paid for her trip and was always nice to her. However, he didn't refrain from saying nasty things to me in front of her because she couldn't understand it anyway. I don't know if that was entirely true, but she had only smiles for him. He even tried to convince me that my mother didn't love me. I told him that was not true but inside I questioned if there was truth in that. I think he got a kick out of it, knowing that he could treat me badly in front of my Mom. The whole thing made me furious. One because Frank could get away with treating me horribly and two, because she just ignored it. I hate to be negative again about Mom but as far as I could see, I didn't see a backbone. If it was good for her, she always blew with the wind. The whole NSB deal was proof of that. She took the easy way out and my father went along with it. It sounds like I didn't love her; I did, but that love came with a lot of baggage. After a long stay, I was so relieved to see her go.

Han Ebbelaar and Alexandra Radius the couple I had danced with in Holland came to New York to dance with American Dance Theater. Out of the small handful of my friends that Frank allowed me to have in my life, they were the ones he really liked. They could come to our house anytime and joined our business dinners very often. I loved that because I had a good time when they were there. Their feelings about Frank were not mutual because they saw the real Frank a couple of times. They stayed in New York for two years before returning to Holland to dance. When they left I missed them very much as we had become very close friends. We saw them on our visits to Holland, along with Phyllis, of course. She was one of Frank's favorites. Phyllis was good looking and I knew men found her very sexy. Maybe Frank thought he had a chance with her. Rudi and Toer never told me what they thought of Frank but Frank was not crazy about them. I think he was jealous of the closeness between us.

We also visited my good friends Walter Nobbe and Hermanus Berserik and his wife Mien. They were painters and I loved their work. Frank liked their work too thank goodness, and bought a couple of their paintings for the apartment.

Frank wanted to show off his new house and I didn't blame him. We now had his parents come and share the holidays at our house. I loved making those special holiday dinners and still do. We entertained more than ever and more entertaining meant spending more money. I talked him into giving me two twenty dollar bills so I didn't have to ask him all the time. He agreed but still questioned where the money was going. I started to write down whatever I was spending including thirty-five cents for subway tokens, or ten cents for bananas. It was all written down so he could see where it went. I would put it under his nose every time he questioned me. I was always surprised when he called the liquor store and placed an order for more than eighty dollars without blinking an eye. If money was no problem, why make it so hard for me?

Maybe it was because I started standing up for myself a little more and he felt he had to do something about it. In any case his behavior towards me became worse. On one occasions I was standing around with a couple of his business buddies at a Christmas cocktail party at our house. The conversation was something about the differences between women and men, and Frank jokingly said while looking at me, "Every woman has a price." I could not resist and said, "Oh really and what is your mother's price?" I saw his face getting angry and he said," My mother does not have a price". The men around us started to laugh and one said," She got you there". He started to laugh too. He could not tell me off in front of his friends, but I felt good giving it to him for once.

I had been upset with him already that evening because he had been flirting with some woman. They were sitting cozily together laughing. Every time I looked in their direction I felt a stake in my heart. I don't even know with whom she had come to our party. This had happened before when we were living on Fifth Avenue. A mystery woman showed up at one of our cocktail parties. I think he felt he could get away with asking his latest flames to the house when there were too many trees to see the forest. This time when everyone had left, he told me that he and that woman had had a lot of fun seeing me upset about their flirting. I guess he punished me for what I had said about his mother after all.

Many evenings after dinner he said, "Why don't you get us some ice-cream at Baskin and Robins". I was happy to do it because I liked ice cream still as much as ever. That was until I found out why he wanted ice cream so often. I left to get the ice cream but forgot the money he had given me for it on the kitchen counter. When I came back for it, I heard him talking on the phone behind the closed door of the bedroom. I listened for a while and realized he was talking to a woman. This whole ice cream business was a scam to get me out of the house so he could make his lovey-dovey phone calls. I was angry and was not afraid to voice it any longer. I went in and told him off, I was so angry I could have hit him. Of course he denied everything, but I was done being made a fool of.

I tolerated all this nonsense from Frank for over six years and had reached my breaking point. I paid enough for all what he called "my mistakes." He couldn't bear that I was changing and said drastic things to try to shake me. He told me, "If you don't like it, you can get a divorce," after I gave it to him about some dumb complaint he had about me. Another favorite line of his was, "I can ship you back to Holland." I actually didn't know what to do or where to go. I felt trapped and he knew it. Going back to Holland was out of the question for sure. Here I had no family or money to fall back on. He did not change but I had. I was not afraid to tell him off anymore, because of that I heard the word divorce very, very often.

I had developed painful ulcers over the years and was on medication all the time. I felt terribly alone and unhappy and had no idea what I could do about it. Where could I go without any money? The two twenty dollar bills would not get me far. I had to do something to get some money saved in case I saw a way out. I put one dollar away every day by adding it to the grocery bill in the little book, and when I thought I could get away with it, I took a little more. Groceries were getting very expensive for him. I would walk many blocks if it meant that I could buy things cheaper and put more money away. The more I could add to my savings, the better. I also added some of my Christmas and birthday gift money from him and his parents. This saving behind Frank's back became my hobby. I was angry with myself for not starting this a long time ago. The process was slow, but it felt good to do something for myself. I was afraid he would find the money so when I had saved a certain amount I sent it to Han and Lex in Holland, who opened a bank account for me. I didn't want to do that here, because I was afraid the bank would send statements to my house. It was crazy to think that I lived in this upscale apartment on Park Avenue, wining and dining the high society business world of Manhattan, but felt poorer than when I was living in my little rented room in The Hague.

Sex was sporadic, either he got it somewhere else or the gimlets had killed his sex drive. In any case when it did happen he would have some comments to make me feel inferior by attacking my self-esteem. My looks were his favorite put-downs. His cousin's daughter had a very large nose and he told me that she was going to have it operated on. I said that I thought it was nice of her parents to do this because I could understand that she was not happy with her nose. His question to me was, "Would you like to have your nose taken care of the same time as hers. Maybe if it is the two of you together it will be cheaper". I thought my nose was okay at that point but even now, I think my nose is a little too big because of that comment.

I did realize that Frank had very low self-esteem and would take his shortcomings out on me. While it was sad for him, it was killing me slowly. I had run out of caring.

Brian was accepted into The Dalton School. This is a very

prestigious school, where children are only accepted if they are a genius, or if their parents are part of the high society of New York, or a child of a famous actor or celebrity. Brian was now five years old and I was told by the school that he needed more male attention. Frank had not much interest in him and that came out when Brian had a meeting with the school psychiatrist. I told Frank what the school psychiatrist said to me, and because it came from a professional person and not from me, he listened. He started taking Brian on Saturday mornings to the New York Athletic club. Better late than never! And he started to realize what a great little boy Brian was. I was so happy for Brian that he finally had a Father who started to care. Brian had learning disabilities, and had difficulties with reading and writing. The school recommended a specialist to help him with reading twice a week. On the days in between I had to work with him on the homework the reading specialist gave me. I was only able to do that with many made-up games because his attention span was very short. His reading improved tremendously, but he never managed to get his writing well under control.

My days were busy, taking Brian to school and to his after-school activities. Then there was the shopping and cooking for the dinner parties. I had to make sure the house was clean, because Frank would inspect with a white cloth looking for dust. God forbid if he found some. He would go on and on about what a bad housekeeper I was. Yes, I was much stronger standing up for myself but he was still able to make me cry. What upset me very much was when he looked under the bed with a flashlight for dust. I told him how angry that made me, and that I was his wife and not his maid. It always ended the same, "If you don't like it, you can get a divorce."

THIRTY-NINE

Christina

Frank had met a Dutchman named Kees who worked for KLM and found out the airline needed electrical work done. Frank thought my Dutch background might be an asset to secure the job, so he invited Kees and his wife over for dinner. I didn't think much of it other than the usual business dinners but this time with a Dutch twist. Our dinner parties typically consisted of six to eight people, but this time it was just the four of us, and that was a good thing.

Fortunately we had a lot in common, and hit it off right away. They knew my painter friends in Holland and Kees's wife, Christina was the sister of the well-known painter Kees van Boheman who I had always admired. They also were friends with the family of my friend and former colleague Toer van Schaik. That dinner with Kees and Christina was a thousand times better than I had expected. We had so much to talk about. It was the start of a long friendship that would eventually be instrumental in changing my life.

Kees and Christina owned a house on the beach in Sea Bright, New Jersey, where they went every weekend and for the summer. They had invited us to their shore house. I jumped at the offer, I could not wait to see them again! Thank goodness Frank thought they were great people as well, and not just because they were good to know for business, although Frank did do some work for KLM. I became very close to Christina and when summer arrived,

Brian and I spent a good amount of time in Sea Bright, more than a week at times. I didn't have to cook and entertain business associates in New York for a while which was a nice reprieve for me. Frank was fine with our departure since it allowed him freedom to do as he wanted and without the worry of me seeing whatever he was up to. At this point in our relationship I didn't care anymore about him fooling around with other women. While vacationing in Sea Bright, I could be myself and felt a freedom that I had not felt for a long time. I counted there, people listened to what I had to say.

There were often lots of interesting people, including Christina's daughter Anita and her husband who also lived in Sea Bright. They had two children who became Brian's playmates. What I remember most about the beach house was the large round table in Christina's kitchen. That table was the heart and soul of the house. A table of countless conversations, long heated discussions and an abundance of laughter. And who could forget the many delicious dinners that were devoured amongst the good company. Kees often made a wonderful Indonesian dish called "Rijst tafel." Its translation is Rice table and consist of many spicy vegetable, meat and egg dishes, and the spicier the food the spicier the conversations. Naturally, there was quite a bit of drinking with a bottomless amount of liqueur, beer and wine. It was actually pretty messy sometimes. It reminded me of paintings by the Dutch painter, Jan Steen. This was the purest form of loving life, something I hadn't felt since I was dancing and when I first came to New York.

Frank joined us on weekends and drove us home on Sunday night. I was sorry to leave my friends and I think he could sense that. On the way home he would bring up some minor thing that I had said about him or to him that weekend that had made him unhappy. When I told him not to make a mountain out of a mole hill he would throw back his famous divorce line.

FORTY

Stephen

Socially Brian was fine, he had after school play dates and took a karate class weekly. People always say that they feel sorry for children who live in the city. Well I can tell you that is not true, there is so much for kids to do and see in New York. Two afternoons a week Brian was picked up from school to go to Central Park to play sports with his buddies. The New York Times advertised things offered by theaters and museums for children to do on weekends and in the summer there were day camps in and out of the city to attend.

Since Frank was a member of the NYAC, Brian could go to their day camp on Travelers Island that summer. They had a great program, which including swimming, archery and running that piqued Brian's interest. It was also very convenient; the club picked him up at eight in the morning and returned him home again at four in the afternoon. Brian would come home with stories about what fun he had and how he especially loved the running races. Brian had mentioned that he was winning those races because of Steve, his camp counselor. Throughout the summer, Brian talked incessantly about this counselor and running. I was happy he was having such a good time and winning those running races. Such a boost for his self-esteem.

When Brian had camp we only went to Sea Bright on weekends. It was so much easier to be with Frank there because he was more likely to hold his tongue in front of our respected hosts.

Although once he made a comment saying I was too skinny to be sexy. When Christina heard it, she got so angry with Frank and retorted, "Are you kidding me, if she clicked her fingers she would have a man for each of those fingers." From then on Frank was very careful with his words about me in front of our friends.

By this time Christina knew what was going on in my life, had seen it for herself and had heard about his behavior. The strange thing was that I didn't tell her things in tears, but told it as if it was a joke. I think I started to look at my situation from the outside in and was beginning to see the absurdity.

At the end of the summer, Brian's camp came to a close. Parents were invited to come and enjoy the last day festivities with their children. I looked forward to thanking this counselor Steve, for all the time he had spent with Brian. Surprise, surprise, what a handsome guy this Steve was. I politely thanked him with a smile and he responded with how much he had enjoyed Brian's company. He asked if he could see Brian some time. Of course I didn't mind. Brian had talked so much about him, I was sure he would like to see him again too.

Indeed Steve called to make arrangements to see Brian. We had a long conversation because he was taking Brian and before doing that I wanted to know a little more about him. I also remembered how good looking I thought he was. Maybe I wanted to know more about him because of that as well. I looked forward to seeing that tall man with the chestnut curly brown hair and the biggest brown eyes again. On Brian's return after spending an afternoon with Steve, Brian told Frank all about the wonderful time he had that day with Steve. Frank always had tickets for sports events to give to clients and said to ask this guy if he wanted to go to an ice hockey game. I was happy to call him. He certainly was nice and I wanted to know more about him. I knew already that he had been on the crew team in college and continued with the sport by rowing races for the NYAC. They gave him the opportunity to become a counselor that summer so he could earn some extra money. He had gotten a science position at a Catholic High School in Yonkers that fall so that ended his rowing career. His parents lived in Yonkers and for the time being he lived with them. I called Steve up and got his mother on the phone. She knew all about Brian and myself. We had a nice chat before she put Steve on the phone.

A few days later, Steve called to thank me for the tickets Frank had given him and we could not get off the phone. He asked me about my background and when I told him that I had been a dancer, he said he had never seen a dance or a ballet. It just so happened that Christina and I were going to see John Butler's *Carmina Burana,* at City Center. I asked if he would like to join us and he said yes.

Christina already knew all about Stephen. The two of us had been pondering about how old he was. After seeing the performance we went to a Greek restaurant called Wine and Apples on 57th Street. Christina conveniently claimed she was tired and went home. We sat there talking until I thought I had better go home before Frank started wondering where I was, Frank was fast asleep when I arrived at our apartment. This made me happy since so much was racing through my mind but none of it had to do with Frank.

I did all the usual things that were expected of me, cleaning, cooking and entertaining but my mind was somewhere in Yonkers. I guess Steve had the same trouble, because he called me saying he wanted to see me. After giving him a drink with some crackers and pâté, the small talk didn't work anymore. He took my hand pulled me to him and we could not let each other go. I looked in his eyes and got this incredible warm feeling I hadn't felt in a long time. It was scary, wonderful and overwhelming all at the same time.

Did I feel guilty about cheating on Frank? The answer was a big NO. Our marriage vows more than seven years ago had been completely meaningless. I had done everything in my power and more to make it good. I felt I deserved this happiness but didn't know how I was going to handle all of this. Only two other people knew what was going on in my life, Christina and Willemien. They were very supportive and I was so happy to have them as friends. When we didn't go to Sea Bright for the weekend, Frank was still taking Brian on Saturday mornings to the NYAC for their father-son time. Steve and I wanted to see each other and Willemien was kind enough to let us have her apartment on the mornings Frank and Brian were out. Lying was the hard part. I did tell Frank that I was at Willemien's, but of course it was a half-truth. One Saturday morning when we left Willemien's apartment walking hand in hand, a foreman of Frank's company passed us. I knew him and he knew me. A quick glance and I saw his surprised face when he saw me hand in hand walking with a stranger. I kept on walking and gave him no clue that I recognized him, wishful thinking that he would think he was mistaking me for someone else. The next days were torture. I had no idea whether or not Frank would find out about the incident. A bomb could explode any moment. Why was I so stupid to be walking hand-in-hand? A week went by and then another. Nothing happened. I am glad I didn't see this man after that anymore, but in actuality I could have hugged him for keeping his mouth shut.

What made the whole situation even more difficult was that Frank's other son Richard came to live with us. Now I didn't have to deal only with Frank's nonsense, but also had a moody teenager to deal with. I didn't eat or sleep much. The only peaceful time I had was with Brian or my phone calls with Stephen. I didn't take any negative talk from Frank any longer. He knew I had nowhere to go and I heard his famous, "Do you want a divorce?" all the time now. To the point that I said it before it came out of his mouth.

FORTY-ONE

Good Friends

I distinctly remember a weekend many years ago because it was yet another major turning point in my life. We had brought Richard to his mother's home for the weekend. Frank decided we should have dinner at a Chinese restaurant that Sunday evening. It was a cold damp January evening and I had not dressed appropriately. We had parked the car far from the Restaurant and I was cold to the bone when we arrived there, but eating my favored sweet and sour chicken dish warmed me up in no time. Brian had a lot to say during dinner because he had been to a friend's Birthday party that afternoon and was still excited about all the fun he had there. We sat at a round table in this typical Chinese looking place when at the end of the meal I said something not to his liking. Again something so minute, but I recall it had something to do with a fortune cookie. Next thing I knew Frank was spewing his divorce request for the umpteenth time. I had hit my breaking point and in response bellowed the loudest *YES!* in history.

Frank almost fell off his chair. For me, it was as if the biggest weight had been lifted from my shoulders. I was floating. "Yes" had flown out of my mouth before I had thought about the next step in leaving my life with Frank. One thing was crystal clear though, I was never ever going back on my decision. I was not going to take his shit anymore, or anybody else's for that matter. I didn't know what was going to happen with me and Steve, but this part of my life; Frank and his controlling, unloving nastiness,

I was completely done with. That fateful night I was shaking when we left that restaurant and this time it was not from the cold. We went home without speaking a word, went to bed silently, and the next morning Frank left for work with the silence still hanging about us. I usually refrain from foul language, but that morning I showered Christina with profanity when I called to tell her what had happened and released a storm of anger that I had pent up toward Frank.

It must have been about ten o'clock that morning when Frank called me. He said he had worked it all out; we would rotate and have Brian a week at a time. Frank probably thought I would be crying by now and saying how sorry I was, but he was SO wrong. I told him that was not going to happen; I was going to have Brian. He said that he knew a big shot lawyer and I would not have a say in the matter when he was done with me. Frank further berated me stating that I was not even an American and the lawyer would arrange for me to be shipped back to Holland. "OVER MY DEAD BODY," I shouted with such conviction I surprised myself. With that Frank hung up the phone. I was trembling with anger but at the same time very frightened at what my immediate future held. I was sure he was coming home and I certainly did not want to be there. Although he had never hurt me physically before there was always a first time for everything. My fear was that this new turn of events could definitely spark such a thing.

I grabbed my coat, phoned Christina and asked her between sobs if I could please come to her house. My only other option was to hang out in the street which did not seem appealing. On my way to Christina's house, I called Steve at his school from a payphone. I was informed he was teaching a class and could not be disturbed. I left a message with the school to have him call me at Christina's. Christina embraced me with a warm, comforting hug at her doorstep and reassured my most impending worry that Brian and I could stay with them as long as needed. I was so thankful to have such a sincere and good friend like Christina in my life. When Stephen called he reinforced Christina's words, telling me not to worry about what Frank and what his famous lawyer could do. Hearing his voice and reassuring words calmed me a little. While updating Christina on the events that occurred over the past twenty four hours, I realized I had no clothes for Brian or myself. I was afraid to return home but thankfully Christina said she would accompany me. I thought to myself, Frank would not hurt me with my friend there.

We drove to the house in anxious silence not knowing what or who awaited us. I never packed a suitcase faster in my life. I felt like I was fleeing my old life, something I wanted to do for many years. Thankfully we were able to quickly and safely retrieve what we needed and return to Christina's house without a problem. Once I started to settled down a bit, my thoughts went to my dear son Brian. I had brought him to school that morning and he had no idea about the changes he was going to endure. I had to cry every time I thought about that. There was no way I would ever go back to Frank and I didn't know how Brian would take that. Being eight years old now he and Frank had finally become closer and I didn't want our divorce to scar their relationship. Later that afternoon Frank called Christina to see if I was there. He wanted to talk to me. I didn't want to hear any more of his ideas or plans for me and Brian, so I refused to speak to him. I had enough to think about for one day.

It was time to pick Brian up from school, I feared telling him the news about our new situation. To my surprise all he said was, "Where are my toys?" I told him he would still see his dad and his toys, but he could also take some to Christina's house to play with. His reaction was such a relief to me, I felt an invisible weight lift from my shoulders, I had not realized how tense I had been about this piece of our soon to be divorce puzzle. Brian had always been a very easy going child, life to him was always so happy-go-lucky. Sometimes I felt like shaking him. I wanted to see some strong feelings or reactions from him, at times I wondered if he had emotions.

Late that afternoon, Frank called again to talk to me. Reluctantly I took the phone after Christina insisted I do so. To my surprise he begged me to come home. When I told him that was not happening, the real reason came out why he wanted me home. Frank asked what he was going to do with his son Richard and what to feed him for dinner that night? Angrily, I told him to get him a pizza and slammed down the phone. Frank always limited my spending money all those years so he could control me, what he did not count on was my good friends who would help me out in the end.

Christina was a great help and supporter, but Steve was very much there for me as well. I told him that I didn't know what was going to happen with us. One thing was for sure, I was not going back to Frank. That fateful "YES" had finalized everything for me. I had meant it with all my heart. Steve professed his love for me and said if I wanted to get rid of him, I would have to throw him out of a window. He was sure about his feelings for me and would patiently wait until I was ready to marry him. I told Stephen to wait with those words. He agreed but gave me three months. I knew Stephen's feelings were sincere, I knew from the moment I met him and his actions from that point forward solidified it.

Stephen came to 106th Street in Manhattan every weekend when Kees and Christina were staying in Sea bright. One weekend his car had broken down and the only way to get to me from Yonkers was to run. To me, that was love in a true sense. Although I had strong feelings for him as well, I was a little worried about our age differences. I just had turned thirty-five and he was twenty-four. When we were together it didn't bother me at all but it was not something to just push away.

It was a terribly confusing time in my life. I felt bad for Brian. After all, I was disrupting my little eight-year-old's life, which was hard for me to deal with. It felt selfish. Frank wanted Brian for the weekends and Brian wanted that as well, so naturally I agreed. Frank called Christina's house constantly, begging me to return home. He even sent flowers and an expensive nightgown from Lord & Taylor. Frank tried so hard that even Christina felt sorry for him. I told her he had many years and opportunities to be nice to me, it was too late now.

Little Kees, Christina's son, also went to the Dalton School. He was a senior and took Brian to school in the morning's and I picked Brian up in the afternoon's. We did this until the end of the school year. In the early mornings the boys argued over the use of the toaster. There was an old toaster in Frank's house, and I needed some more clothes for us anyway and thought I would pick them up at the same time. It was strange going back to the house again after leaving on that emotional morning. I didn't belong there anymore and was happy about it. Uncomfortable being there, I rushed around gathering what I came for. In my haste, I had forgotten to put away the step stool I had used to retrieve the toaster. When Frank came home he probably thought I was emptying his house out. When I went back again to gather more personal items from my closet, the locks had been changed. Did he think I was taking things of incredible value out of the kitchen cabinets? If I wanted to do that, I would have taken a painting.

FORTY-TWO

Lawyers, Lawyers And More Lawyers

Through Christina, I hired a female attorney who represented me in family court so I could receive child support from Frank. All of the court procedures took time, I was happy and relieved to have the money I had saved over the last couple of year. This whole event happened right after my birthday, so I still had the money Frank and his parents had given me for that occasion. I also had Brian's savings account that I could use for the time being. Luckily I had been in charge of that. Eventually, the court ordered him to give me $100 a week. I gave Christina $75 of that, it was the best I could do at the time.

Frank's lawyers suggested we see a marriage counselor. From my standpoint it wasn't necessary, since I was never going back. My lawyer said it was a good thing to do so the court could gather my side of the story as well. The counselor wanted to hear what we had to say separately first. She asked me what brought me to the point of wanting a divorce. It was as if she opened the door of my soul. I purged everything that had been boiling inside of me for the past eight years and cried my eyes out while doing so. When I was done I felt an overwhelming relief. All the poison was out of me, as if a kind of cleansing had happened.

Next it was Frank's turn to meet with the counselor. She had probably recorded our sessions and then had to make an evaluation. A few weeks passed before we were asked back to the counselor for a joint session. Frank picked me up and we headed to the meeting together. He even tried to hold my hand in the taxi. I pulled it away quickly, holding his hand was the last thing I wanted to do. Initially, we were seen separate again. When the counselor asked how I was doing, I replied, "Much better since our last meeting." In response, she laid out her recommendations; I can work with him and maybe he will be able to make things somewhat better. Do you want him back under these terms?" I replied firmly, "I don't think so." Her eyes met mine and I saw she understood me and my situation completely and answered, "I don't blame you. So we are done".

My lawyer was going to try to get me more support money. She inquired about Frank's salary and if he had stocks and bonds. I knew he had some stocks that also had my name on it, but how much they were worth I couldn't tell. Frank's salary was as much of a mystery as it was for her, I had no idea. My attorney reassured me not to worry, she would dig and come up with the figure. When she came back with Frank bringing in three hundred and sixty-eight thousand dollars a year, I could not believe it. This would be a sizable income today, so one can imagine what it was worth in 1974. This was his reported income, but it probably was more because big companies have loopholes. To think he made such a big deal about giving me two twenty-dollar bills? Wow, how generous of him!

Frank had the best law firm in the city representing him, and had told them, and my lawyer, he was not even going to give me an ashtray. He could keep his ashtrays I didn't smoke anymore anyway. After living with Christina for five months, the court awarded me four hundred and fifty dollars every two weeks from Frank. Those hot shot lawyers could not do anything about that. I never had that much money to spend in a month.

FORTY-THREE

Scarsdale

With this money, I was able to afford an apartment for myself and Brian. Stephen was still living and working in Yonkers. I wanted to be close to him, so when I found a beautiful Tudor-style one-bedroom apartment in Scarsdale, a town in close proximity to Yonkers, it was settled. Brian and I had nothing when it came to household items, so I bought a small butcher block dining table, a bed for Brian, and a mattress for myself to put on the living room floor. Stephen's parents were kind enough to let me borrow four folding chairs and gave me some kitchen utensils. We were now on our own and our new life had begun.

I enrolled Brian in school and considered the possibility of teaching ballet. There was a shopping center across from our apartment complex. The center had a large food store and a couple of other shops including a karate school. Karate and ballet require the same kind of space, maybe their schedule had some open time slots which would allow for me to teach ballet. Determined to make my plan work, I went to talk to the owner. Much to my surprise and fortune, I was informed that the Karate studio was now used as a Weight Reduction business which only required a small room. The larger space was available and the perfect spot to teach my classes. I was ecstatic and the owner was thrilled to be getting additional rent money. A win , win situation for all parties, things were falling into place. First finding my apartment close to

Stephen, then this very convenient center with the perfect space for me to begin a business. I could see my future changing in a positive way.

With the addition of some walls, mirrors and some advertising, my Ballet Studio was up and running even if I had only one student in a couple of my classes. I needed to have patience and that paid off after some months. I only worked three days a week because I had to think about Brian needing my time as well. He even did a couple of ballet classes with his friend Jason, but they were there mostly for fun. I loved teaching even if it wasn't financially very rewording. I reached back into my own childhood remembering the influence my former older colleges had on me. I wanted my students to have a little touch of that as well and took them to performances. Netherlands Dance theater and The National Ballet would perform in New York ones in a while and my eleven and twelve year old students loved going back stage and see the dancers up close. I hope some will remember that.

Stephen's parents were concerned that their son was involved with a married woman. I have to be honest, that was not the only reason they were worrisome. Our age difference was unsettling as well. I was eleven years older than Stephen. I was sympathetic to their concern and could understand where they were coming from. Poor Stephen had to deal with the brunt of it since he lived with them, but once they saw us together, they saw that the love between us was real.

Frank was still in the picture since divorce proceedings were still ongoing and not finalized. He was up to his usual dirty tricks once he realized I was not coming back to him. One Saturday afternoon, Stephen arrived at the back door of my apartment, something he had never done. When I questioned why, he replied, "Because someone is watching the front." Brian was at Frank's for the weekend and we had plans to go to the movies that evening. We snuck out the back and peered through the bushes to see if anyone was still watching. There certainly was someone watching, but not very incognito. I hope not all private detectives are as worthless and incompetent as this guy. For fun, Stephen went up to the detective and asked him for the time. He had no idea that the joke was on him. We were laughing then, however the next day when he followed me, I was very disturbed by his presents. I was done with Frank and his controlling, all knowing ways, so I called and sternly asked him to get his spy off my back.

While divorce proceedings, Frank, the investigator had been consuming me and my time, I also had Brian at the top of my list when it came to worrying. We struggled daily with homework. He didn't listen to a word I said and was unable to work for longer than ten minutes. I tried to have a serious talk with him, but afterwards his only response was, "Can I go play now?" Frustrated with his aloof response, I felt sorry for him all the same. Brian had not done well at The Dalton School and in this current school he wasn't doing any better. The school had suggested that Brian attend a school which specialized in learning disabilities. I hated doing this but I had to ask Frank for financial help because I could not afford eight thousand dollars a year tuition for this special school. Frank said he would think about it and would let me know. I really needed expert help because Brian's disabilities were too big for me to handle. Schools today are much different, back then schools didn't have special education teachers. Brian's school had a psychologist but I think she did him more harm than good. She said Brian wanted to do his work sitting on top of her closet and so she let him. I can imagine Brian enjoyed this immensely. He loved climbing and was always ready to explore and have fun but I didn't see how this was helpful. I actually thought it was flat out stupid.

Once again I was at a major crossroad in my life and had to make another hard decision. Frank came back with a complicated deal which I had to consider. If he paid for the special school, he wanted custody of Brian. I despised the idea and shed many tears because of it. I went back and forth with my decision and discussed it endlessly with everyone close to me. Was I selfish to say no to Frank because I would miss Brian too much? Yes , but my selfishness would deny Brian of the help he needed most. I was put into a no win situation and detested Frank for having this power over me again. I came to the realization that Brian should have a say in this decision. Even though Brian was young, I wanted to know his feelings on the matter. To my sadness but also to my relief, Brian was fine with living with Frank full time. For Brian, the only difference was that he would come to me on weekends instead of the other way around. So in the end, I reluctantly gave into the deal because it was best for my son. I was secure enough in my relationship with Brian and knew that a simple piece of paper stating who had custody would not change how Brian and I felt about each other. Frank really cared for Brian now and I didn't think he would cause him angst by making it difficult to see me.

Frank's attorneys informed him that leaving me with nothing in the settlement could not happen. The apartment on Park Avenue was put in my name as well. My lawyer was persistent in raising the small amount of money that was offered to something more substantial which let to numerous negotiations. I felt that this could go on endlessly and was exactly what Frank had envisioned. All I wanted was a conclusion, a settlement, and more so my freedom from Frank. To me that was more important than any amount of money. I instructed my lawyer to tell Frank's fancy attorneys that I was fine with the forty thousand dollars they had offered. Frank said that he was unable to pay this all at once. Yet another one of his tricks to delay this process and possibly still get the outcome he wanted. I had an answer to that; If he was so short on money I would happily accept the forty thousand allotted to me in three installments. No longer would I back down to Frank and his little tricks, I deserved this much and was determent to succeed in some way through this.

A court date was set for the beginning of August. Papers were drawn up stating I wanted a divorce because of indifference. I could have gotten the divorce for abuse but did not feel the need nor want to purge the ugly truth to a group of strangers. With that, our marriage was over and I was finally free from this man who had made a portion of my life miserable. I told Frank once Brian began attending the special school he didn't have to pay me alimony anymore. The only contact I wanted with Frank was regarding Brian and his wellbeing. Brian stayed with me until the middle of August and we did a lot of talking, or at least I did. I had a difficult time letting him go to live with Frank, but Brian was very matter of fact about it. It was a character trait of his that I never understood. I had never seen Brian show much emotion but he would get upset with me if I showed any. He went to Frank and prepared for his new school. He was back in his old home again, the only difference was a new house keeper, a real one, to take care of him.

FORTY-FOUR

Wedding Bells

With all the stress and angst over the past couple of months, I needed a break. Brian had left for a vacation with Frank. So Stephen and I decided to do some cheap camping excursions around the country before school started again. We picked up a well-used two person tent from Kees and Christina that they didn't want any more. The tent must have been twenty years old because it was made of a heavy material that was no longer used. After some simple packing and preparation, we filled up Stephen's little car in Yonkers and we were off. Sitting in this car not knowing what adventure laid a head of me, I felt freedom as if I finally could breathe fresh air after a long time. My new life had begun and I was the happiest person alive at that moment and could not stop laughing.

The first night of our adventure, we put the tent up and discovered a gaping hole. At every subsequent camp ground, we became the laughing stock of our neighbors and we laughed with them. On top of our sorry looking tent, we affixed a piece of plastic to cover the hole as best as we could. Our camping neighbors had tents equivalent to one bedroom apartments complete with porches. I didn't even know they made such fancy camping stuff! Since our funds for the trip were meager, our diet consisted mostly of spaghetti and fruit. To conserve money on camping fees, we sometimes just stopped on the side of the road and slept in the car. Camping definitely provided many new experiences for me. Once we were further West, we had the company of all sorts of animals at night. I was unaccustomed to the howling coyotes or was ever concerned about the presence of bears. For this city girl, those animals were meant for the zoo, not my nighttime companions with only a flimsy tent to separate us. I have to admit, I felt much safer in the car at night. Even the day time brought on new experiences with animals. During our hike in the Grand Tetons, at the trailhead there was a drawing of a bear with blood dripping from his mouth and claws. The sign informed hikers to make a little sound by talking so people wouldn't startle a bear. Scared to death that we would encounter one, I talked for two hours straight on that hike.

Typically when visiting a big city or town, we would stay in a cheap hotel. During one of those economical stays, entering our simple room and seeing mirrors on the side of the bed and on the ceiling we quickly realized it was a place where people came for an afternoon delight. You could see yourself from the back, to the front, and double. All that for eight dollars a night! You can't get a better deal than that.

Upon returning from our camping adventure, I was supposed to see Brian. I phoned Frank to make plans to pick Brian up, but was informed that he had made other plans with Brian for the weekend. I asked to speak with Brian since I wanted to hear for myself what he wanted. Much to my dismay, Brian wanted to stay with his father. My heart ached with his decision. I missed Brian terribly and had not seen him in over two weeks. I think it is easy to change a child's mind if you dangle a carrot in front of them. Suddenly I realized that that little piece of paper that Frank now owned was more powerful than I expected. Knowing that now, would I not have given him custody of Brian? No, because Brian's future depended on all the help Frank could give him. What I didn't realized before was that whatever happened, or what Frank wanted was okay with Brian. Frank had enrolled him in a school that would deal with Brian's problems and that's what was most important.

It seemed like my life was moving in two directions. My old life with Brian and Frank was moving in one way with me on the outskirts, while my new life with Stephen was moving forward in a positive, healthy way. Upon returning home from vacation, Stephen moved in with me. Finally, I had a wonderful loving relationship and felt I was given a second chance at happiness again. I was thirty-six now, young enough to start over but a lot older than Stephen. He was not at all concerned about our age difference. Stephen loved me and wanted to marry me. I felt the same and could not see my life without him anymore. Lucky for me, I did not look much older than him, my concern was how that could change in the years to come. Would we look ridiculous together when I am sixty and he forty-nine? Our love was too powerful and I was too happy to let something like a number interfere. My thought was whatever happens years from now; I will take care of it then. Therefore, I made the decision to live in the present and accept this happiness, for it was what I needed most.

We set our wedding date for December 27, 1975. Something small and intimate, with Stephen's closest family and relatives, as well as my mother and some friends. Christina was my maid of honor and Stephen's father Dominick was giving me away. That alone speaks volumes for the wonderfully close relationship I had with his family. Jean, Stephen's mom, and I did all the cooking for the wedding. We hired a couple of people to help with the serving, and rented some tables, chairs and silverware. The wedding was held in a beautiful small, old Catholic church in Scarsdale. We had met the priest beforehand to select readings. There was one I rejected immediately, something about God taking a rib from Adam to create a woman. I was done being the underdog and wanted to be equal with the man I was marrying. I had no religious background or beliefs. To get married in the church, we had to promise to bring our children up catholic and since we were living together, not to consummate the marriage until after we were officially husband and wife. I don't want to go into details but we had a lot of fun with that one.

Stephen and I at our wedding.

With the first payment from Frank's divorce settlement, I opened a bank account which earned ten percent interest, and the bank give an electric can opener as a thank you. The money earned would eventually go towards our future house. Lack of money was still the story of my life. I was still teaching ballet but didn't have many students, so that income was not substantial. Stephen went to teach in another Catholic school and now made a whopping sum of seven thousand, five hundred dollars a year. Our rent was two hundred and seventy-five dollars a month, which was covered by one of the two paychecks Stephen received monthly. The other check and whatever I made was for everything else. There's a Dutch expression, "You row with the oars that are given to you". In other words do the best with what you have. In actuality, I enjoyed the challenge of making ends meet and was already good at it because of my life with Frank, he had taught me well. While I was still receiving payments from Frank, I bought an inexpensive Sears sewing machine. With this machine I made curtains and pillows from sheets for our apartment. I also fashioned some clothes for myself and even made a pair of jeans for Stephen. We eat a lot of pasta made a hundred different ways and I even baked my own bread. Our birthday celebrations were going to a pizza parlor and having a large pie. Life was simple and I could not be happier.

I needed a wedding dress and found a beige two-piece one for fifteen dollars. It was kind of lacey and I think it looked stunning on me. On our wedding day, I carried a bouquet of pale pink roses, and had tiny roses throughout my hair which was up off my face and neck. I was the happiest person in the world when I entered the church on Dominick's arm and saw Stephen at the altar's edge waiting for me. When the priest started to speak, we realized he was not doing the reading we had chosen. Stephen and I looked at each other quizzically. We soon realized he was reading the passage with the infamous line about Adam's rib. It was hard to contain our laughter at this simple blunder when we realized that the priest had switched our wows with another couple. They must have been disappointed not hearing the Adam's rib part, or maybe only the groom was.

FORTY-FIVE

Eleuthera

Stephen and I really wanted to go on a honeymoon. We had some money from our wedding, as well as some of the money I had sent to Han and Lex in Holland to keep for me. Little did I know when I was saving that money that it was going to be used for my honeymoon. Life is really unpredictable. We eagerly headed to a travel agent and asked for the cheapest, warmest vacation spot they offered. They had something on the island of Eleuthera in the Bahamas. At the time Eleuthera was basically beach, sun, sand and nothing else. Our hotel was just a bar with a couple of guest rooms upstairs. Our room could not have been more romantic. It was small and simple, with a petite terrace adjacent to a large tree covered with exotic vines climbing all over it. The hotel was not directly on the beach but since it was so intimate, the owner drove us there each day. He picked out a very secluded cove we had all to ourselves, and I did something I had never done before, but could not resist doing on this beautiful beach with the love of my live. I went topless.

If we planned to have dinner at the hotel, we had to let the owner know that morning. One day we went fishing and I caught a nice size fish. We gave it to our hotel owner who said he would prepare it for us. He actually didn't charge us for dinner that evening, because he said we brought our own food. This gives you an idea of just how laid back the place was.

There was not much business on the island, but to our surprise and delight there was an ice cream factory. We discovered it when we rented a motor scooter for a couple of days to explore the Island. Our favorite daily trip was going to the ice cream factory to get a half gallon of ice cream to split. We had to eat it all at once because we couldn't save it, and throwing it away was out of the question.

New Year's Eve fell during our stay there, so we inquired about any special celebrations. There wasn't much tourism except for one all-inclusive resort. Luckily the resort had dinner and dancing planned for the evening and we were able to attend as outside guests. Fully dressed in party attire, we hopped on our motor-bike to the only tourist party on the island. A long table, covered in festive hats and noise makers, ran the length of the dining room. Many people were already seated when we arrived but we were able to find two open seats across from each other. As I settled into my seat I glanced up at Stephen and knew immediately what he was thinking. Why did we come here and what did we get ourselves into? I tried to make conversation with the people around us but it was more a job than a pleasure. They all knew each other and were talking about things that made sense to them, but not to us. They talked about their experiences that day, and in the middle of the story they were laughing so much that we never heard why it was so funny. Stephen was very shy when he was young and small talk was not something he enjoyed. I had a hard time not laughing while watching his face struggling with this uncomfortable dinner. We were so relieved when the dancing began and were released from the prison table. We danced for a while, but eventually danced ourselves right out the front door. We never made it to midnight, but it was a very, very happy New Year.

FORTY-SIX

— ∞ↄℴↄↄ∞ —

A Bundle of Joy

Stephen constantly tried and finally got a job in a public school that payed more money. Now we were able to look for a house. We found a lovely small house in Somers, NY that sat on the end of the road on a hill. With the move, I had to give up my teaching in Scarsdale, but it was the right time anyway because I was pregnant. I was 39 and needed to have an amniocentesis. When I finally got the call that everything was fine, we jumped for joy. Not only was the baby healthy but it was a girl! Either sex would have been perfectly fine, but because I had a boy already, I was delighted that it was a little girl. Stephen's parents, Jean and Dominick were overjoyed. They had Stephen and his older brother George, but had hoped for a little girl long ago. We gave them that wish in the form of a granddaughter.

On August 21 at six in the morning, we became the parents of our baby girl. Her name, Tatiana, was a big to-do with Stephen's family. I always liked that name ever since seeing Russian dance films with Rudi. Dom asked me, with a face that told me that I should rethink it, "What kind of a name is that, I never heard of it?" He asked Stephen a couple of times, "What's her name again?" We had fun quizzing him after that to see if he remembered. Once she was born her name came out of his mouth with only love and affection. Then there was Granny, Stephen's grandmother. She lived in an Italian neighborhood on Arthur Avenue in the Bronx. Like many residents of that section

218

of the Bronx, she didn't speak English very well. We must have repeated Tatiana's name to Granny a million times, but she never got it. After a while we gave up and let her call her whatever she wanted. Don't ask me why but she called Tatiana "Batsiaan" for the rest of her life.

I loved Stephen's family and I knew the feelings were mutual. Jean was not the typical Mother-in-law; she was one of my best friends. I had the privilege to be part of this warm, loving family, and knew how lucky I was. They were Italian-Americans. Sunday dinners together with the extended family were huge and lasted for hours. Dom sat at the head of the table with cheeks as red as the wine he was drinking. When he was very happy he treated us to a couple of Neapolitan songs. Jean was the matron of her whole extended family. She had two sisters and a brother and they were all married and had children and grandchildren. The Sunday get-togethers were mostly at Jean and Dom's house. After dinner the men and kids played touch football, while the women cleaned up and got things ready for phase two, the desserts. Everyone brought all kinds of Italian goodies and the table would be full once again. It didn't end there, phase three consisted of making cold cut and eggplant sandwiches to take home. God forbid anyone went home hungry! It was an underlying, understood rule, you had to leave their house stuffed and content.

The first year of Tatiana's life I devoted all my time to her. It was one of the happiest years I can remember, but at the same time I had an itch to start teaching dance again. I thought maybe this would be possible to do in the public school of the town we lived. I made an appointment with the primary school principal, Mr. van Tassel. During our conversation, I discovered that his family name came from the island of Tessel, a small island in the north of Holland. It just so happened that my maternal grandmother came from the same island, and just like that an instant connection between us. Needless to say, Mr. Van Tessel was very happy to have me set up a dance program at the school.

Twenty-two years later a new principal didn't think of it as something beneficial to the students and that was the end of that lovely program.

FORTY-SEVEN

On Everything Comes An End

My connection with Singel 99 came to an end when Mom had a stroke and could not live alone any longer. We went to Holland to empty out her house, and when everything was gone, Stephen and I slept on the floor. Lying there, I saw the brown walls from years of smoking and the outlines of pictures and things that had been hanging on them. The rug still had dirty imprints as if the furniture was still standing there. The place was all lived out and forlorn.

It was the last time I set foot in the house; that had been home for twenty-seven years. Since then, whenever I am in Amsterdam, I always make a point to go there, and look at it from across the canal. I imagine Rie and Frits on the first floor and my younger self walking up to the third floor, and I am there again.

Sometime later Mom had her second stroke. When I visited her hospital bed, she knew who I was, but could not speak and had little control over her arms and hands. She wanted to say something and it seemed to be important. She pointed to her wrist. I thought she wanted her watch or her pocketbook. Whatever I thought she meant was a no with only a slight shake of her head. I gave her a pen to write it but she could only scribble something I couldn't make out. It was very frustrating and after a while she was too tired to continue. Sadly, I never found out what she was trying to say.

She moaned and was obviously hurting. I asked the nurse if

they were giving her some pain medication and she replied they were not. When I questioned this, the nurse abruptly answered, "You have to ask her doctor." This ended up not being a simple task and required me making a formal appointment that was for a day and a half later. By then I could see that Mom was in terrible pain and wasn't responding to me any longer. I was already very upset seeing mom in pain, and when I finally got to see the doctor, she sat authoritatively behind a large desk. She spoke with a chic accent which immediately turned me off. The doctor explained that if she gave Mom pain medicine she would not be able to see how much damage the stroke had done. To me, that didn't make any sense. What was apparent, was that the doctor was not taking into consideration the physical and emotional needs of her patient's wellbeing. I asked her if she thought Mom would ever get better and she simply responded, no. Then why would she wait to give pain relief to someone who was dying? In the end, I made progress with the doctor because they immediately starting giving Mom medication. I knew it was helping because I saw Mom's face had relaxed, as did mine because at least I knew she was no longer suffering.

While I was in Holland, the director of the old-age home where Mom had been living let me stay in her small studio apartment. It was Saint Sinterklaas time in Holland, so when I turned on mom's television a special Sinterklaas variety program was airing. It was laced with Sinterklaas songs, songs I had not heard in years which flooded me with memories from my past. The time fleeing our café, our time in Germany, life on the boat and the whole NSB situation. I was overwhelmed with emotion in this place that had been abandoned by Mom. I felt like I was a little girl again in need of her mother. The program was hosted by Mies Bouman, the wife of the producer Leen Timp who I had worked with on television programs and I had danced and acted in his film *Mouvement De La Hollande* that was choreographed by Rudi. The film had won a prize at the Cannes Film Festival. This brought back even more memories but this time about the end of the film when I walked into the North Sea in full costume and toe shoes.

The dance film Mouvement De La Hollande, which won honorable mention at Prix D'Italia film festival in 1960.

Lying in Mom's bed, I gazed around the room and thought so this is what Mom looked at every night before falling asleep. There was a big picture of Brian, who Mom and I took care of together when he was an infant, amongst her many little knick-knacks, one stood out immediately. It was the copper ashtray I had made in school, which seemed like a lifetime ago. Being in mom's space so intimately, the flood of memories of my life and knowing that I was facing my last goodbye with my mother was all too upsetting. I could not stay in that room one more night.

I sat by my mother's side the whole next day in the hospital. I talked to her about Brian and Tatiana, and even some trivial things like the weather, hoping she could hear me. Once in a while she would suddenly open her eyes and look at me. Before I could say, "Hi Mom", she closed them again. It was terribly disappointing and heart wrenching. I called Willy and Jaap and asked them if I could stay with them. They lived close by in an old typical Dutch farmhouse with their two children. I was so glad to be with them in the evenings. Their hospitality and company was such a reprieve from my difficult and emotionally draining days in the hospital with my mom who was slowly slipping further away.

Three weeks later on the day after Christmas Mom passed away.

FORTY-EIGHT

Fate or Coincidence

My ballet school that I had opened in nineteen-seventy-nine was a success. Both Stephen and I were making more money, and felt it was time to look for a bigger house. We bought our next family home from a German couple in their late sixties who had moved to America after the war. Both of them changed their first and last names, something I found very fishy if you had nothing to hide. Did they have a secret as well?

We had sold our little house but could not move into the new home until a week later. Since we were in limbo, we arranged to store our furniture in one of their garages. I asked if I could bring some of my plants in the house since the garage was too dark and cold in March. While carrying them in, a little water from a plant's saucer spilled on the slate floor in the hall. Quickly, I ran back to the garage to fetch a towel to clean up the spill. Upon returning to the hall, the German owner was looming on the top step with hands on his hips and snarled, "What the hell are you doing to my house?" At first I thought he was joking because his reaction was much too harsh for a minuscule puddle of water. Much to my surprise and disdain, I soon realized his anger was not in jest. My initial reaction was to tell him off, but changed my mind. The house was not ours yet and I certainly did not want to jeopardize it. Ten minutes later he was normal again and showed me his gardenia plant that had produced a flower. He carefully took the flower in his hand and while fondly petting it asked," Isn't this beautiful?"

His behavior triggered war time memories, and on a small scale he was very similar to how the SSers had behaved in the war. They were the people who could say something sweet to a Jewish child to keep the mother calm and then close the door of the gas chamber behind them. Only a few minutes prior, he had scolded me like I was dirt and now I had to admire his dumb flower. The war had followed me once again, what a coincidence. If I had told him that I had been an NSBer he probably would have embraced me. The whole encounter and series of events bothered me so much. The last thing I wanted was to be connected with those two Germans. It brought me too close to my secret again, a secret I had buried for many years within me. A neighbor later told me that the couple used to have a German Shepherd (no surprise). The husband had taken the dog to the back yard and made his little son hold the dog while he shot the animal dead in the head. Another disturbing tidbit I discovered about them, they had an intercom located in the master bedroom, which allowed them to hear everything that was going on in the guest room. They were in my eyes the scum of the earth.

FORTY-NINE

It Is What It Is

Owning a ballet studio and teaching dance was thoroughly fulfilling. My life was full and happy. Stephen and I had a wonderful loving marriage and our daughter who was growing into a beautiful woman. Tatiana was the perfect combination of the two of us. Curly, dark chestnut hair and brown eyes from Stephen and the bone structure of her face and long lean body type from me.

Years later, I showed a picture of myself at eighteen years old to my grandchildren. When I asked who they thought it was, they all shouted in unison, "Mommy!"

As for Brian, he finished college, is happily married now and doing well. I do not see him often because he lives in Michigan.

Frank, who I would occasionally see on special events, was getting very forgetful and not much with it. All of his heavy drinking had probably affected his brain. He had terrible back pains and needed a walker. The last time I saw Frank he was completely bent over. When he saw me he tried to make himself as straight as possible which must have been very painful. I felt sorry for him. I had forgiven him by now, and didn't want to dwell on the past. At age eighty Frank became very ill and passed away.

My in-laws, Stephen's parents, Jean and Dominick were retired and drove to Florida for the winter months. They did this until 1995. That year we stayed in our summer house on Harbor Island in South Carolina for New Years. My past came to haunt me as I walked over the dunes to the beach and three military jets flew low over my head. Without thinking, I dropped into the sand because there was nowhere to hide. I surprised myself with this reaction, realizing I had not let go of the defense mode from my past. I thought how lucky I was to now have a beautiful beach house on a lovely island and more importantly to have my wonderful family to enjoy it with.

Jean and Dom were going to stop by our beach house for a couple of days before continuing on to Florida.

I was all ready for their arrival when the doorbell rang. Looming in the doorway was a policeman who told Stephen to call his brother immediately. We instantly knew something was terribly wrong.

"Dead, "both of them?" Stephen asked his brother George in utter disbelief. They were instantly killed in an accident caused by a woman who had fallen asleep while driving.

George could not handle the loss of his parents and fell into a deep depression, for which he took heavy medication to numb his feelings. Two years later George passed away from a heart attack on his birthday. He never got over his parents death.

But in life there are always new beginnings. For our family this new happiness came with the news that Tatiana was getting married.

We were elated for her and this wonderful news. Stephen and I were also relieved that she was going to settle down because our little social butterfly had given us one too many worries during college and the years immediately following. We looked forward to her settling into a life with her new husband. She now had someone who would look after her, and Kyle was the right person for that. I made decorated pouches filled with white covered almonds, an Italian wedding tradition that made us feel that Jean and Dom were still with us. On all special occasions, they are always at the forefront of our memories.

Tatiana became a mother of three, and I am as close to

those children as if they were my own. Alexa, Hudson, and baby Harrison are the loves of my life. I melt as they run into my arms calling out, "Grandma!"

FIFTY

Anniversary

There was a special occasion coming up, the 50th year anniversary celebration of *Netherlands Dance Theater*. It was going to be a big event with people I had worked with and who I had not seen for years. Rudi and Toer I had seen many times over the years. I had seen more of Rudi because he had been in America and Canada setting his ballets for various companies. We would always coordinate a visit during those times. The hotels or apartments where he stayed were big enough for me to stay too. Many times he also would add some days so he could spend some time with us at our house. On one of those occasions he saw a book I had. It was called "The New Book for the Youth," and had been one of my precious possessions since I was little. It was given to me by a woman when I lived on the house boat. Being a child of the war as well, Rudi said, "Oh, they gave that to you too?" I simply nodded yes and froze. I would have liked to ask him why we got it, but I was afraid it had something to do with my secret. The thought of Rudi finding out I had been a NSBer would have killed me even after all these years.

Rudi, always conscientious of right and wrong, would come to the aid of anyone – human or animal – if he saw mistreatment or injustice. I could certainly never share my secret with him.

We were very close and talked often on the phone during happy and sad times. Rudi was not going to be at the Anniversary event because he was not feeling well. He had been treated for breast cancer and was never the same after that. He was too weak and also didn't like to be surrounded by so many people. The statement he had made about his parents not coming to the premier of Night Island was that they were people shy. He had the same problem; he would get very shaky when he had to leave his house.

After arriving in Holland early in the morning, the day before the big event, I went to Willie's house in Haarlem for a wonderful relaxing day and evening with her. The next day I took the train to The Hague and had a hard time remembering how to walk to the company's theater. It is funny but after forty years away from a city, you have a hard time remembering how to get from point A to point B, especially when things have been rebuilt so much. I asked a woman in the street for directions. After showing me the way, she said, "Much success tonight." I realized everyone knew about this special weekend event.

Having no other place to go, I made the office of *Netherlands Dance Theater* my temporary home and dressing room. I brought a black dress and after trying to look the best I could, it was time for me to pass the television cameras. Peering through the office windows, I saw Hans van Manen had been cornered for an interview when he arrived at the theatre. A smile grew across my face as I watched my old friend with all his mannerisms still in place as the Hans I remembered. I descended the stairs and as I passed the cameras, they did not finch nor pull me aside. They don't even question MY importance I thought with a smile. Upon entering the large theater hall, I did not see anyone I knew. I grew more uncomfortable and nervous until I saw a waving arm belonging to Han Ebbelaar. He had clearly seen my panicked face in the sea of people. Most of the old timers where standing together, some I hadn't seen for thirty years. It was wonderful to see Mabel, who was one of the Ants. We had so much to catch up on but after just a quick glass of wine and a little nibble, we had to take our seats in the theater. Everyone had to be seated before Beatrix, the Queen of Holland entered.

The event was really special for us. All the former rebel

members of the company, minus Carel Birnie and Aart Verstegen who both had passed away, were individually recognized by name. We each stood for a round of applause during our accolade, something I had not expected to happen at this event. Another pleasant and unexpected surprise was meeting the Queen during the intermission. We were personally introduced to her. After the introductions, Hans van Manen turned to the Queen and stated, "Hannie was the tallest dancer in Holland." I retorted with, "Well at least I am famous for something." Everyone burst out laughing and yelling, "No your feet, show them." I never thought of asking the Queen if it was okay to slip off my high heel in front of her, but in one quick moment my foot was bare and being shown to the Queen. The Queen's responded politely, "Yes indeed, very nice for dancing." When everyone else left, I continued telling the Queen what an honor it had been for me when we were invited to her Parents' 25th wedding anniversary after performing for them. Her parents were the Prince and Queen, and I questioned myself if I'm allowed to say parents or do I have to say "Her Majesty Queen Juliana and Prince Bernhard." Too late, I said it already. That is what you get when you are not use to speaking to a Queen. We had a nice talk about our grandchildren and talked about what they wanted me to bring back from Holland for them. She was going to Mexico the following day and I wished her a pleasant trip.

After the performance, Han and Lex drove me back to Rudi's house in Amsterdam for the night. I just had to see him while in Holland. The uncertainty of ever seeing him again after this visit was heartbreaking. My trip, coupled with the honorary dinners with many old friends, made me realize the importance of these friendships and how I must try my best not to let so much time pass between seeing and talking to one another. Our physical distance apart from one another definitely hinders this, but since that trip back to Holland I am happy to report we have stayed in contact.

After everything was over, I was going to stay in Rijswijk with my nephew Hans for a couple of days before returning home. I looked at the evening news on television and saw Queen Beatrice inspecting the guard on the side of the president of Mexico. I realized that when I wished her a nice trip I had seen her as a Grandmother who was going on a holiday and not like a Queen doing her royal duties. Royalty or not, she is a person with an extended family like everyone else.

This trip was very emotional as it dredged up so many memories. I thought about my life on the Singel with my parents and their friends Rie and Frits. Rie had passed away about four years prior. I had stayed in touch with Frits for the first couple of years after Rie's death, but then lost contact. Guilty and upset with myself for letting that happen, I felt since I was here in Holland I should make an effort and go visit Frits. He had moved from the Singel to an apartment. As I made my way to his apartment I pondered if he still resided there or even worse, was alive. I was thrilled to see his name on the door to his apartment and was greeted with his smiling face. Thankfully, my visit was very timely because the next day he was moving to an old age home. I had a lovely visit with him reminiscing about the past and it made us both feel good. I left with his new phone number and promised to call once I was back in the states and he was settled.

After talking so much with Frits about my parents, the Singel years and the occasion of *Netherlands Dance Theater's* fifty-year anniversary, I felt as if my whole life raced through me. And of course, there was still my secret, only Stephen and Tatiana knew about that. Years earlier I had blurted it out to Stephen in tears. Much to my surprise, he had accepted it as not a problem at all. Presently, I fully believe he truly feels that way. However, early in our marriage right after I told him, I felt that every time he got upset with me about something it was because of the secret. Telling him was not planned at all. We were on our way to Canada to visit our friends Bonnie and David Young. While potato farms blurred on either side of the car, memories from the war leapt into my head and I began telling Stephen how Mom and I would dig up potatoes. Naturally, he started to ask questions and one thing led to another. Before I knew it, my secret had flown out of me in an emotional explosion. In the end, I was overwhelmingly relieved he finally knew. I realized Stephen didn't have much knowledge regarding the N.S.B., just like most Americans. Stephen and Tatiana tried to shake me of my guilt, but that was difficult to except. You cannot let go of something that easily when it has followed you your whole life. Keep in mind, my daughter and husband didn't know how bad the N.S.B. had been for Dutch people. It was bad enough to take away the Dutch citizenship of my parents and it took a long time to get it back. Tatiana said she had talked a little about it with her husband, Kyle. I made her swear not to delve any further about my secret with him. I was worried Kyle might research this group further and be disgusted by me. It was very difficult for me not to think that people would whisper to one another, "That is the woman who was with the Germans in World War II."

I had not thought about my birthplace for many years and wondered how it looked now. I asked my sister Henny if she was willing to take me to the Apeldoorselaan. I didn't want to go alone and she said she didn't mind driving us. I don't know why but my stomach was fluttering like it was filled with butterflies. I hadn't been home in seventy years. The moment we got there, I recognized it immediately. While standing there a sea of memories flooded over me. I gazed up at the second floor window where I had fallen in love with dance. Much to my surprise, I see a large sign, "Dance School." My interest was piqued and I know I could not just turn my back and walk away from this. I had to find out what this school was all about. I climbed the stairs quickly to find the door locked. While standing at the locked door telling Henny how disappointed I was, the owner came up the stairs and asked if she could help us. I explained that not only was I born in this building but also it was here at her Dance School where I had gotten my first dance lessons so long ago. She said that she didn't mind letting me in so I could take a look.

Netherlands Dance Theater 50th Anniversary. These are some of the dancers who started the company. From left to right: Gerard Lemaitre, Marianna Helarides, Hanny Bouwman, Marianne Westerdijk, Johanna van Leeuwen Sepe, Martinette Janmaat, Mabel Alter, Milly Gramberg, Annemarie Verrhoeven, and Charles Czarny.

One of the last times Rudi and I danced *Night Island* together.

The owner had forgotten something and returned to fetch it. Was this a coincidence? I entered the room that had shrunk in my mind but to my astonishment, had the same looking floor. The door to our apartment was gone but I knew that behind that wall was where I was born. Tears welled up because at that moment I realized my life had achieved a full circle by standing in that room. The two women were staring at me most likely bewildered at my emotions. Understandably, they didn't know everything that had happened here and the enormous impact that had on the rest of my life. My first dance lessons triggered my love for that beautiful art form which in turn saved me as well as shaped me into the person I am now. If it wasn't for dance I would not have been standing in that very room wearing every emotion.

Upon reflection, I asked myself, who had guided me to visit Frits just at the right time? That dear friend had passed away when I called the home two weeks later. Who had made me think of going to the Apeldoorselaan and who had made the owner return at the same moment I was standing forlorn against the locked door? I believe it was my mother who wanted me to realize that although she had done some things wrong, it had all turned out right for me in the end. It was because of dance, it had become my savior so long ago. I had been very fortunate to become involved with some very gifted and inspiring people in the dance world. People I admired and loved, who helped make my secret bearable. It had been dance that had forced me to verbalize my own Night Island by dancing my guarded inner secret when I was sixteen. Back then I could not tell it to anyone, it was only for everyone to see. Now it is for everyone to read about it if they so choose. Finally, I am emotionally ready to share my life history and my secret. I forgive you Mom.

THE END

Brian

When Brian went to live with Frank, he settled back into his former home with ease. Stephen and I picked him up every other weekend and Frank cooperated for the most part. As well as attending the new school, Brian also saw a specialist once a week to help him. I have to give Frank credit for doing everything in his power to help Brian be successful. After completing elementary school in the city, Brian attended a boarding school in Connecticut and then went onto college at Fordham University. Things had worked out for him and I was grateful to Frank for that.

When I asked Brian how he felt about changes or happenings in his life he always answered, "Fine." His curtness was something I was used to since he was a small boy. Now that he was an adult, I was still unable to have a conversation about his real feelings. He just wouldn't open up. If I ever showed emotion about something, he would get very upset and push it away. No matter how hard I tried, I could never get through to him. Therefore it was hard to know the real Brian or maybe that was all there was. He was fun to be with, easy going, very likable, and there was an incredibly pure innocence about him. I never heard him say a bad word about anyone. People truly loved him. Throughout his life, his friends always spoke highly and fondly about my sweet Brian.

Brian passed away at the age of forty-six after a two-year battle with colon cancer. He never complained about his illness, and enjoyed every day right until the end as if everything was normal. Even during his last days under hospice care, he watched the history channel as if nothing was wrong. That was Brian, don't make waves. He had told everyone not to be upset," After all 'fun' is in the word 'funeral'." That was Brian.

At the funeral service there were so many people in attendance, there were not enough seats for everyone. Brian had coached a soccer team of seven-year-old girls, something he loved doing and could not stop talking about. I think it was the same for them because the whole team came to the funeral in their uniforms honoring the coach they loved. At the end of the service everyone in the church was invited for lunch. There was a big hall with tables and chairs set up for everyone. All food and refreshments were made and bought by Brian's friends. It was a celebration of Brian's life. I cannot describe my feelings at that time or even now, because words are not good enough. There are also no words to explain the way you feel when you lose a child, it is too overwhelming.

Fly-fishing was a big part of Brian's life, and he even made his own flies. Whenever he could, he would be with some friend on one of the many Michigan Rivers doing what he loved. Catch and release of course, he could not harm anything. Near the end of his life when he was heavily medicated with morphine to relieve his pain, his arms would go up and his hands made imaginary flies. When he did that, I felt he was in a good place on a beautiful river or lake fishing into eternity.

I love you my sweet Brian.

www.ingramcontent.com/pod-product-compliance
Lightning Source LLC
Chambersburg PA
CBHW031246090426
42742CB00007B/337